VALUES
AT
WORK

D1714315

VALUES
AT
WORK

The invisible threads between

people, performance and profit

MICHAEL HENDERSON
&
DOUGAL THOMPSON

Harper*Business*
An imprint of HarperCollins*Publishers*

A very special thank you to all our clients for your commitment and belief in your own people. In particular, thanks to Steve Phillips, Bill MacLeod and Peter Dalton for their support when the going was tough.

Paul Chippendale has provided invaluable expertise on values theory, and has been a generous sounding board and mentor.

Thanks to Shar, for continuing to hold the vision of what this is all about.

Cartoon on page 10 used with the kind permission of Malcolm Evans.

National Library of New Zealand Cataloguing-in-Publication Data

Henderson, Michael, 1963-
Values at work : the links between people, performance and profit /
Michael Henderson and Dougal Thompson.
Includes bibliographical references.
ISBN 1-86950-471-2
1. Business ethics. 2. Industrial management—Moral and ethical aspects.
I. Thompson, Dougal, 1955- II. Title.
174.4—dc 21

HarperBusiness
An imprint of HarperCollinsPublishers

First published 2003
HarperCollinsPublishers (New Zealand) Limited
P.O. Box 1, Auckland

ISBN 1 86950 471 2

Set in Garamond 11.2 pt
Printed by Griffin Press, Australia, on 80 gsm Bulky Book Ivory

You don't have a choice whether
your organisation works with values.
You do have a choice in how.

Contents

Introduction

And beware that you don't fall into another kind of error;
the folly of those who wear out their lives in ceaseless business,
but have no aim on which their action or thought is based.

Marcus Aurelius Caesar

Every organisation has values, whether it consciously realises this or not. Those organisations that understand their values can guide their own destiny and create for themselves a sustainable competitive advantage.

As we approached the new millennium there was an upsurge in interest in understanding the nature of values and their impact on people, performance and profit. Many business books of this era make at least a passing reference to the importance of values in business.

However, values-based management is sometimes greeted with scepticism. Why? Many people have worked in companies which have gone to great lengths and expense to determine their values. Having created a set of values, management then busy themselves pitching those values to their employees and engraving the values onto some type of ornate plaque to be hung in a commanding position in the reception for all to see and admire. The values are usually articulately expressed, impressive to behold, inspiring to read, compelling in purpose and captivating to the heart. People hope these values will somehow represent the truth of the enterprise's nature, but unfortunately this is not often the case. The poetry, art, philosophy and spirit embodied in the words come up short when compared with the day-to-day realities experienced by people within the business. The values are seen as hollow and meaningless, as nothing more than the most recent offering from yet another senior management retreat.

Is this disbelief justified? Often, when we spend even a little time comparing a company's stated values with its actions, behaviour, dialogue and systems, we rapidly draw the conclusion that values are not generally practised as part of the day-to-day activity of the business. The elegant phrasing doesn't give birth to waves of morale washing vibrantly throughout all levels of the organisation. The fine words aren't referred to as part of all decision-making processes. They don't provide the framework for the company's culture. They are a lie, or at best a misguided wish list.

Organisations, having invested all this time, money and effort into defining their values, are simply getting it wrong.

Why? Is it that values are not really as important as the business leaders and academics would have us believe? Are values nothing more than the latest business guru's sales pitch, or the moralistic, philosophical ravings of new-age greenies who quite frankly wouldn't know a successful business if they tripped over it?

Our experience and research suggest the answer is that many organisations simply do not know why or how to successfully create and align values within their businesses.

We believe values are important. In fact, the very definition of values suggests they represent or are drawn from what people believe is *most important* to them. Even if an organisation claims not to operate using values, the reality is that it *does* — it simply hasn't recognised that the various priorities and preferences exhibited through every decision within the company is a reflection of the underlying values at work within its culture.

Companies do not spend too little time on defining their values. In fact, companies typically spend *too much* time crafting their values, but nowhere near enough time on the equally important task of aligning their business activities with the values they've just recorded.

Why did we write this book?

After many years working with organisations seeking to implement values-based management, we wanted to create a comprehensive guide explaining why and how implementing values improves both a company's business results and its employees' experience of work. This book also seeks to debunk some common myths regarding the nature of values within business, and provide clarity on what values are and how to make them work with organisations. Our knowledge and experience come from our work as values consultants to corporations, individuals and sports teams over the past decade. This experience has given us insight into what does and doesn't work when applying values to business. Many of these insights are common sense, and yet we often find they're not common practice in business.

Our experience indicates that values have a central position across all facets of business — financial, strategic, operations, marketing and human resources. Values are the most common and fundamental link between these areas. To ignore the values relationship between people and their work is to guarantee mediocrity in performance, fulfilment and quality. For example, many quality-assurance initiatives within businesses have failed simply because they didn't take into account the influence values have on people in the business. It's one thing to expect and measure quality; it is another to have it as a true value — to have it because people in your organisation have a personal belief in it. People need to feel personally committed to quality, not just obliged to provide it. As a result of this commitment they find their work more meaningful.

People want and need meaning in their lives. They want values at work.

PART ONE

Putting values and business into context

The degree to which an organisation's values are deliberately chosen and embodied by its people directly influences the degree of success the organisation can expect to experience in achieving its objectives.

More than any other concept, [values are] an intervening variable that show promise of being able to unify the apparent diverse interest of all the sciences concerned with human behaviour.

Milton Rokeach, *The Nature of Human Values*

CHAPTER 1

Demystifying values

Business people don't like to talk about values. But without them, all business is about is making money. To me, achieving business goals is great. But no business goal is worth sacrificing your values.

CEO Patrick Kelly, PSS World Medical

—

What are values?

Values are the sum of our preferences and priorities. Preferences are what we would rather have in our lives than do without. Priorities indicate how important each preference is in relation to another. A value can therefore be described as a preference, multiplied by its priority.

Preference x Priority = Value

Values capture and express what is important to us — in life and in business. They are abstract concepts represented by words, which if they are to have any real meaning, must be experienced and lived rather than just written and talked about. Values are not physical objects — for example, money is not a value, but the things it represents are, such as security, wealth, power and freedom.

Values create focus. When we identify our values, we can then direct our efforts and attention into what we have decided is important. This is like looking at a star-filled sky, and picking out a particular constellation — there are lots of areas in which we could focus our efforts, but the important ones will shine through from the rest. When an organisation clarifies its values and deliberately focuses on what is most important, it allows everyone in that organisation to focus their efforts on those chosen areas.

Values also enable us to begin to understand our underlying motivations, beliefs and assumptions. For example, if we consider a value to be like the eighth of an iceberg visible above the waterline, then the large area out of view represents our underlying beliefs and assumptions about why the value is important. If an organisation selects profit as one of its values, the beliefs underlying this value might range from 'We need to provide a return on investment to shareholders' to 'We need to keep head office off our backs' to 'We need to be able to pay our employees'. These beliefs are important because they create an emotional connection to the value and they influence the priority we place on it.

A company that has a preferred way of doing business or operating has, by definition, a set of values on which it operates. If a company does not have a preferred way of doing business, then this is in itself a preferred way of doing business. Either way, the company has a set of values by which it operates.

Here are some preferences that may relate to how your company operates:

- Economical and successful
- Mission- and objectives-driven
- Profitable
- Growth- and expansion-oriented
- Quality conscious
- Responsible to the community
- Efficient and well planned
- Research- and knowledge-focused
- Customer-focused.

How many of these preferences can you relate to your organisation? Were they easy to identify? Did they stand out as obvious and familiar aspects of your organisation? If so, you've just identified some of your organisation's values.

When we present this list to executives on our Values at Work seminars, they're often surprised to realise the business practices they hold in such high regard are in fact values. A typical comment is, 'I always thought values were soft, touchy-feely things, not hard-core business fundamentals.' It's at this point of the seminar that people begin to realise that the conscious application of values may have something to offer them.

As the rest of the workshop unfolds, it becomes apparent to the participants that the degree to which an organisation's values are deliberately chosen and embodied by people directly influences the direction and degree of success the company can expect to experience in achieving its objectives, goals and strategies.

Values need not be as business-focused as the so-called 'hard' values listed above. 'Hard' and 'soft' elements referred to in business are all values. The hard values such as profitability and productivity are a result of other things such as synergy, loyalty, commitment, passion, service and ideas, all of which are soft values. You don't get the hard stuff in business without the soft stuff.

Appendix 2 lists 125 globally recognised values, developed by the Minessence Group, a network of qualified values consultants who share their research and resources to support one another and their clients to act in alignment with their chosen values. The Minessence Group is also responsible for accrediting values consultants and ensuring that ongoing research keeps up to date with global and regional trends in values development. The list of values is referred to throughout this book as AVI: A Values Inventory. If you're looking for inspiration when considering your own organisation's values, refer to this list.

Our values principles

When working with clients and assisting them to become values-based, we base our advice on the following nine principles. They reflect our underlying beliefs about what it takes to have values work successfully.

These principles have emerged out of countless conversations with our clients; supporting their endeavours to create better places for people to work has taught us what works best when bringing values to life.

1 Values are the priorities and preferences of individuals and groups, which reflect what is important to them.

An organisation demonstrates its values in its actions, systems, decisions and strategies. The preferences and priorities of an organisation can be identified simply by watching the organisation at work.

2 Unprioritised values create conflict.

Values that have not been prioritised create oscillation. A values conflict such as not knowing whether profit is more important to the organisation than service results in conflicting strategic thinking and behaviour as well as alternating and inconsistent decision-making.

3 An organisation's values are its real leader.

All leaders are led by values. Leadership starts from setting examples and making decisions. Both examples and decisions are a result of evaluations of what will best serve the organisation's primary interests.

4 Values are the DNA of all organisations' culture. They determine what happens and why.

Values provide the embedded codes of a culture. Robert Fritz, author of *The Path of Least Resistance for Managers*, states: 'The values that dominate an organisation will displace other competing lesser values.' A small number of values dominate any culture — it's important to ensure they're the ones that work best to achieve the desired results in a manner that's most fulfilling.

5 Organisations do not put their values into practice, people do.

Because values are only guiding concepts, they still require people to act in alignment with them. If people within an organisation do not support the organisation's values, then that organisation cannot implement its values.

6 Values drive performance.

People will only put their organisation's values into practice when their personal values are in alignment with the values of the organisation.

People will not perform as well as they can if they are working in environments where the company's values conflict with their personal values. Values alignment is the key to performance and productivity. When we know what we want and what we want is important to us, then we are motivated to achieve it.

7 Decisions are based more on values than rational analysis.

Decisions are predominantly made on an emotional basis, with logic then used to justify the values-based emotions. Behind every economic transaction, decisions are being made based on preferences and priorities and hence on values.

8 Values determine quality.

Business places a huge emphasis on quality, with its due diligence, zero defect, money-back guarantee practices. All of this would cease to exist without values, because the ability to create and appreciate quality is fundamentally based on values. Imagine a tradesperson carving wood, welding steel or moulding clay without indicating a sign of preference for a desired outcome of their work, or an accountant placing no priority whatsoever on balancing figures accurately. Consider the ramifications of a heart surgeon who approached the whole exercise with a 'close-enough' attitude. With no clear preferred outcome, the chance of achieving a high-quality result is random.

9 The values at work within an organisation influence behaviour.

An organisation is only as effective as its ability to live its values. Take all the values out of a company for just one week, and by the end of that week the organisation will cease to exist. For any anthropologist attempting to understand a culture, the starting point of any research and observation is always the culture's values. These are identified by studying the beliefs, behaviours, rituals, icons, symbols, actions, systems and decisions of the group. Knowing a culture's values provides meaning and context for its behaviours.

Different ways of describing values

Abraham Maslow, a famous psychologist, suggested values are defined in many ways and mean different things to different people. Discussing values became so confusing semantically that he was convinced we would soon give up this catch-all word in favour of more precise definitions for each of the many sub-meanings that have been attached to it. He may well be right, as a number of commonly accepted terms have come to be used when describing values.

The following descriptions are not different *types* of values; they are simply some different ways of defining the way values are used, lived and referred to. This means that a specific value may fall into several of the following descriptions depending on how the individual chooses to relate to the value. Understanding these distinctions is an important part of demystifying values.

Goal values

Goal values are those that we aspire to achieve. They are future-focused. A well-formed vision statement will contain goal values. An important and defining aspect of goal values is that they are not a means to achieving something else; they are the reward. For example, to experience the value 'competence', other values need to have been acted upon first, such as practice, skill, confidence and planning.

Means values

Means values are those on which we want to focus our attention in order to eventually achieve our goal values. An example of a set of means values might be having the value of confidence in our work if the goal is to achieve quality.

Espoused values

Values that are not yet acted upon are espoused values. They may be articulated, discussed, defined and communicated, yet they have not yet been put into action. This applies to both individuals' and organisations' values.

Aligned values

Aligned values occur when a group of people have similar values and are moving in the same direction. In other words, they experience no conflict in living the values. Alignment of values occurs when an organisation's values are mutually compatible with (but not necessarily the same or identical to) the values of people associated with the organisation. The organisation's values do not conflict with employees' personal values, and people feel their own values are in harmony with the work they do.

When values are successfully selected within the organisation, they will focus the attention and activity of employees, who will willingly apply them. Values and people become aligned with the business' vision and strategic objectives. Values alignment is critical to organisations; without alignment, employees will continue to operate using the values they feel best suit their own needs. Work can become meaningless, and people collapse into lethargy, hopelessness and often become disoriented in their own lives. If the organisation does not provide an aligned values focus for their employees, then employees will provide their own.

Unaligned values

This is a term used to describe two typical situations:

1. when one set of values is incompatible with another set or with other values within its own set.

2. where a set of values is incompatible with an individual's or organisation's overall purpose or identity.

Unaligned values can arise between two individuals or between an organisation's values and its employees or clients. For example, one of our clients discovered the organisation he had worked for over a number of years produced chemicals used in germ warfare. The values conflict this created was so strong that on confirming his findings with the director, he resigned on the spot. An example often raised in workshop discussions on prioritising values is whether people value health and wellbeing over employment, such as working for a tobacco company. Not all unaligned values are this obvious, however. Unaligned values are often difficult to pinpoint, although their presence is indicated by low morale, poor work ethics, complacency, staff conflicts, high stress levels and so on.

Unaligned values occur as a result of differing preferences and degrees of perceived priority being attached to different and potentially conflicting values. Organisations often experience unaligned values when employees fail to put the company values into practice; that is, the dominant values practised in the organisation are not the organisation's values, but those of the employees. This can also happen in reverse where personal values become subverted by the overriding demands of the organisation's values.

When two or more unaligned values have not been managed successfully, the result is a values conflict, where by honouring one value, another is dishonoured or jeopardised. For example, an organisation may list its values as quality and profit. But if it achieves its profit by selling low-quality products to the 'cheap' end of the market, then it is compromising its value of quality.

In *The Path of Least Resistance for Managers*, Robert Fritz notes, 'Without a higher-order organising principle in which the company's aspirations and values are positioned in relationship to its current reality, an organisation will self-organise into various structural conflicts. Why? Because various groups try to do a good job, and so they support the effort they see as the correct one.' This type of values conflict can also occur within an individual's own personal values; for example, someone might find their personal values of 'family' conflict with their value of 'work'. In other words, wanting to be effective at one value may lead to being less effective at another.

Values conflict often occurs between such values as profit and people. In other words, in order to maximise profit, by definition employees are not treated as well as possible. For example, a company may limit a bonus scheme for employees, or free chocolate biscuits may no longer be available, or the telemarketing team might have to work with poor quality furniture because buying more comfortable chairs would reduce the company's profit.

Failure to align individual and organisational values guarantees conflict. There are many ways to avoid this and these are discussed throughout the book. The more familiar we are with our values, both as organisations and individuals, and the more successfully they are aligned, the less conflict tends to occur.

This concept is all the more important for organisations when we appreciate that companies do not put their values into practice — people do.

What values are not

Having defined values, before we venture any further it's important to clarify what values are not. This is important because many people confuse values with other linguistic and philosophical terms, and in doing so confuse and undermine the power of values. Set out below are some common terms that are regularly confused with values and a brief description of our interpretation of them.

Ethics

Ethics are agreed codes of behaviour adopted by a group or association. They are created and adopted by people who are interested primarily in ensuring there are guidelines for behaviour for the group's members. For example, doctors and lawyers have ethical codes of practice, which they swear to uphold as part of their professional practice. An ethical decision is one which typically involves choosing between what you have agreed not to do, and what you now find yourself wanting to do.

Morals

Morals are our adopted viewpoints, pertaining predominantly to what we perceive as good and bad. They define for us the 'rightness' and 'wrongness' of something or someone. Someone who is described as being morally corrupt or lacking in morals, is judged by others as acting, thinking or behaving in a manner that the observer perceives as bad, wrong, evil or inappropriate in some way.

A moral decision typically involves choosing between options: one you believe to be right and the other wrong.

Principles

Principles are agreed-upon time-tested truths, of a natural, scientific or man-made nature. For example, the scientific principle of gravity is one that has been tested over a long period of time and repeatedly demonstrates it operates by the same rules or guidelines and hence is accepted as the truth.

Individuals may have their own personal principles, that is, time-tested, self-accepted or adopted truths they have incorporated as rules to live by in their own lives.

Judgements

Judgements are our defining labels (usually expressed as adjectives) representing our beliefs about something or someone. Judgements usually say more about the person doing the judging than they do about the person or thing being judged. To judge someone's values usually involves having a moral perspective on their values, i.e. to see them as right or wrong. For example, saying someone is 'ugly' is a judgement based on your personal beliefs, and also implies you consider being ugly is 'wrong'.

Attitudes

An attitude refers to a culminating effect of a collection of beliefs about something, a situation or someone. Attitudes are reactive responses to environmental stimuli. In *The Nature of Human Values*, Milton Rokeach writes about the emphasis that has been placed on attitudes over values: 'A major reason psychologists have paid more attention to the attitude than to value concept is that more sophisticated methods have been available for measuring attitudes. This greater availability of methods for measuring attitudes brings to mind Abraham Kaplan's law of the instrument; "Give a small boy a hammer and he will find that everything he encounters needs pounding." All such sophisticated research tools not withstanding, theoretical considerations suggest that values are nevertheless more central than attitudes as determinants of human behaviour.'

Virtues

Virtues are the preferred personal characteristics of something or someone. They are not necessarily the priorities of that person (although they could be).

Virtues are typically the behavioural characteristics of an individual; for example, courage or patience. Although a person might be attributed with great courage or even perform an act of extreme bravery, the value driving that behaviour is unlikely to be a preference to appear heroic. It is more likely that they have placed a greater priority on something else or someone else in that situation than they have on their own wellbeing.

Needs

Needs are perceived necessities. Perhaps the best-known reference on needs is found in the work of American psychologist Abraham Maslow. Maslow suggests that human beings gain their motivation for behaviour from their needs. He suggests there is an ascending order of needs, set out in his famous hierarchy of needs diagram, below. Maslow's hierarchy leads the reader to presume that progress is good, i.e. that being at the top of the pyramid is preferable to being at the bottom.

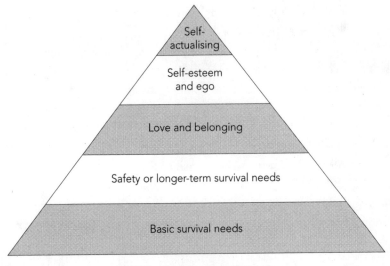

Maslow's hierarchy of needs

Source: Maslow, 1971

The needs towards the bottom of the hierarchy are called basic needs and are associated with our physical existence. The needs towards the top of the hierarchy are considered by Maslow to be values. However, what we value and what we need are often two very different things. For example, when a cigarette smoker says they need to stop smoking because of their health, that doesn't necessarily mean they will stop smoking unless they value their health more than they value continuing to smoke.

If you live in a country where your needs can relatively easily be met, your life then takes on a 'what would I like and want' perspective (a values perspective) far more than one of needs. In other words, once our basic needs are taken care of (food, water, warmth, shelter, company), life becomes more about our personal preferences and priorities than it does about needs. Our values indicate what is wanted, desired or preferred.

Consider the possibility that, in fact, we do not need anything. We do not even need oxygen, unless, of course, we wish to stay alive. If we wish to stay alive, that is a preference, not a need. Is such a comment ridiculous? Surely everybody wants to live? Because suicide exists in our society it is clear that not everyone wants to stay alive. When you look at the rest of your supposed needs, you will find many of them are not needs at all, they are preferences.

Needs are often a means to an end. If I *want* to bake a banana cake, I will *need* the ingredients and an oven.

Another view, espoused by William Glasser, suggests humans only have four predominant needs: love, fun, mastery and freedom. How we go about achieving these four basic needs varies from person to person (again determined by their individual preferences and priorities), so that how one person prefers to gain a sense of loving and being loved may differ significantly from another. The correlation between values and Glasser's interpretation of needs is so strong that the two have been combined to form a comprehensive values inventory process known as 'A Values Inventory'.

A Simple Values Inventory				
	FUN	LOVE	MASTERY	FREEDOM
1				
2				
3				

As a simple introduction into this process, write down in the spaces provided in the table opposite three things you currently value in your life. Alongside these three things, tick any relevant box as to whether you feel it contributes to fun, love, mastery or freedom.

The values that meet all four underlying needs are considered our highest priority values.

Beliefs

Beliefs are very closely related to values. They are in many ways inseparable, yet there is a subtle difference. A value can be seen as what you believe in; the belief is why you believe in it. For example, most organisations value profit. However, why they value profit can vary enormously, which in turn affects how people feel about implementing the value.

Beliefs are critical when working with values. In many respects a value is simply an established belief or set of beliefs about the desirability, preference and priority of something. Like values, there does not seem to be a universally accepted definition of beliefs. In *The Nature of Human Values*, Milton Rokeach suggests, 'A value is an enduring belief that a specific mode of conduct or end-state of existence is personally or socially preferable to an opposite or converse mode of conduct or end-state of existence.' As Rokeach suggests, it is the belief that something is important or preferable that creates the value. In other words, beliefs always come before the values.

In many respects our values are nothing more than a representation of our underlying belief systems. If a particular point of view comprises a number of beliefs that are deemed to have a favourable influence on our life, then the resulting focus of these beliefs emerges for us as a value.

The more underlying beliefs we have attached to a particular concept the higher the likelihood that a value will emerge from our collective attention to that concept. This does not mean we will necessarily value the actual thing on which our beliefs are focused; however, it will almost certainly lead to a value emerging as a response to those beliefs. For example, we may have numerous (and fixed) beliefs about competition. This does not necessarily mean we will *value* competition as a direct result of having these beliefs (although we might). What we may end up valuing is confidence and competence, as we recognise that without these values we may be less effective at operating successfully in the market, so the result of experiencing a perceived threat (competition), leads to the belief that we have to prioritise competence and confidence in our business. Anything we value must have as a prerequisite, a belief that it is important to us for some reason. Likewise, anything we deem to have low or no value is also predetermined by a belief.

Harry Palmer, the author of the insightful book *Resurfacing*, suggests that if you study anything in enough detail you will be studying a belief.

The definition of 'belief' we like to work with is that a belief is our expression of the degree of certainty we have about something. If you ask us if there is water on earth, we have a strong belief there is because of our high degree of certainty. If you ask us if there is water on Pluto, our belief is less strong because we are not so certain.

Our degree of certainty simply indicates that given what we hold to be true (based on logic, facts, assumptions, fantasy, rumour, intuition, experience, information, etc.), we develop a point of view about something.

Obviously our beliefs are not necessarily correct. For hundreds of years it was believed the earth was flat. Now we know it to be a sphere. There are still simpler examples of inaccurate belief systems that we all readily buy into. For example, many people, when you ask them where the sun rises, will tell you it rises in the east. However, the sun doesn't rise at all — what actually happens is that the earth turns on its axis towards the sun, giving the appearance of the sun rising from ground level.

Beliefs are of vital importance when creating values alignment within organisations. They are what finally convince an individual that their personal values will be compatible and safe within the cultural framework offered by practising (or not practising) the organisation's values.

CHAPTER 2

The benefits of values to organisations

Values are essential to wealth creation.

John Elkington

—

If you are looking for a business leader who embodies the values for which their organisation stands, you need look no further than Vodafone Pacific CEO Grahame Maher. In the interview below, he explains the process of how and why Vodafone New Zealand became a values-based organisation and highlights some of the benefits of doing so.

How do you define a values-based organisation?
A values-based organisation is one that exists for some reason above and beyond solely making money.

So what is the reason that Vodafone exists for?
Unlocking the potential of people.

Why specifically has Vodafone committed to becoming a values-based organisation?
Before we arrived in New Zealand to take over BellSouth, we decided that our strategic approach would be values-based in order to successfully and seamlessly make the acquisition easier. The new culture had to be values-based as the criteria for our decision-making.

In what ways has being values-based added value to the organisation?
Our market share in a period of just over two years has grown from 17
per cent to 40 per cent. We have achieved this to a large extent with the
same people in the same market as BellSouth operated. It's amazing,
people love their work, they are super-charged. We have higher brand
awareness and a much higher staff retention rate.

*To what extent do you feel that growth could be directly attributed to
being values-based?*
Possibly as high as 50 per cent. Using values is the only consistently
sustainable way to manage a business. There are huge benefits to be
gained from being values-based. For a start, it gets rid of unnecessary
hierarchy in the business. People are made to feel more involved. It also
means you can move fast. You switch from having to think everything
through to knowing if something feels right or not. It's like being in 'the
zone' in sports. You can achieve results without having to constantly
check how and what you're doing is acceptable. When the values are
clearly defined, people can make informed and aligned decisions on
their own — they're empowered to do so by the values. This means
being values-based unlocks the potential of people. It's powerful. It
enables you to achieve with them what you cannot without them.
People instinctively know what is the right thing to do. We don't need
process and tight hierarchical control to make things happen.

How has the leadership team responded to this process?
Some love it, and some are challenged by it. Some have grown way
beyond my or their own expectations through the values process. On
the other hand, you will lose people who do not fit the values process,
which is a healthy sign for a good values-based organisation.

How has it affected you personally?
The more I am involved with a values-based organisation, the more
challenged I am, and therefore I grow. I have mentors and a personal
balance scorecard to monitor the journey. Values are always a journey,
not a destination. As a leader, I've learned to lead and inspire people to
align their individual values and the organisation's values. I've also
learned that even if you're already technically good at what you do, in

business you still need values if you want to get better. I believe people and businesses operate in cycles. Most die before they are actually dead. You have to be a values-based organisation if you want to be sustainable. The book *Built to Last* [by James Collins and Jerry Porras] talks about this.

Why do you have such a great passion for values?
Values are the reason I am in business, they are why I am a leader. I am totally committed; I believe in this process.

Do you believe other organisations in New Zealand would benefit from becoming values-based?
Every organisation in the world that has people in it should be values-based. I'm often asked if it's so good, why am I talking about it so much. People think I'm giving away one of our biggest competitive advantages. But it's your people who are your competitive advantage, and all people have values. It makes sense to work with values because that's what people do naturally. Besides, it's got to be a good thing for business overall.

So you definitely feel values offer a competitive advantage?
Yes, of course. Especially if the other organisations are not values-based.

Any advice for other CEOs who might be considering becoming values-based?
You're mad if you don't, but don't do it unless you are genuine. It takes personal commitment. If you're not for real, you'll soon be caught out. You've got to be totally committed. It's not an advertising campaign or marketing ploy. This is long-term and deep. You'll know if you're supposed to do it if you'd be prepared to sell your grandmother to get it done. It's hard. It's good fun, too, and worth it, because it unlocks the potential of your people, but it is hard work.

Some business leaders believe that values are too 'touchy feely' — what do you think of that?
They're wrong. They just haven't being paying attention. Our foundation values at Vodafone are what we do. Our inspirational values are how we do it. If they can't see there are different ways of doing things, some being better than others, well . . .

So what is the future of values at Vodafone?

Continued growth, wider sharing of our commitment to values and continuing to unlock the potential of our people. We're also providing all new staff with a values programme as part of their induction to Vodafone. It's exciting. The wider sharing is now starting to encompass our suppliers, distribution and development partners. The theory about a values fit that delivers added value to customers is not only applicable to our staff, but to everyone involved in the delivery of our service applications. As we share these with them along with our strategies, they find it surprising. What I find surprising is that they're amazed that we're sharing it. These values are part of our DNA and it's impossible to be involved in the delivery of our services unless this is clearly understood. When it is, by staff, suppliers and partners, it is very powerful.

Benefits to organisations of becoming values-based

Financial benefits

The most commonly asked question in relation to values and organisations is about the correlation between values alignment and financial success. Grahame Maher clearly believes that values alignment between the company and its employees does create financial success, as evidenced by the increased results after the company became values-based.

Research conducted by the Wilson Learning Center, which surveyed 25,000 employees in 14 organisations in the USA, suggests financial success is strongly correlated to employee fulfilment. In fact, they report that 39 per cent of the variability in corporate performance is attributable to the personal fulfilment of employees. Values alignment between the company and employees is a prerequisite to and the foundation for employee fulfilment.

Perhaps the best-known research on the relationship between values and financial success is highlighted in *Built to Last* by Collins and Porras, which examines the success habits of America's 'visionary organisations'. These high-performing organisations include American Express, 3M, General Electric, Hewlett-Packard, Norton, McDonnell Douglas, General Motors and Chase Manhattan. The significant determining factor that the authors suggest separates these gold-medal organisations from their counterparts is that they possess what the authors refer to as a core ideology: 'This is who we are; this is what we stand for; this is what we are all about.' They define the core ideology as comprising only two component parts: core values and purpose.

Unlike traditional business theory advocates, maximising shareholder return and profit are not what drives these elite organisations. The authors state, 'Throughout the history of most visionary companies we saw a core ideology that transcends purely economic considerations.' This observation is one of the prerequisites of being a values-based organisation. The detailed study showed that these visionary companies were generally more ideologically driven and less purely profit-driven than the comparative companies in the study. However, the authors are quick to point out: 'Of course we are not saying that the visionary companies have been uninterested in profitability or long-term shareholder wealth . . . Profitability is a necessary condition for existence and a means to more important ends, but it is not the end in itself for many of the visionary companies. Profit is like oxygen, food, water and blood for the body; they are not the point of life, but without them there is no life.' This description coincides with values-based organis-ations that recognise that 'what we stand for is more important than what we sell'.

What does stand out about these organisations, ironically, is their financial performance. Collins and Porras provide an example to indicate the level of long-term financial success these values-based organisations have achieved. 'Suppose you had made equal investments in a general market stock fund, a comparison company stock fund and a visionary company stock fund on January 1, 1926. If you invested all dividends and made appropriate adjustments for when companies became available on the stock exchange, your $1 in general market fund would have grown to $415 on December 31, 1990. Your $1 invested in the group of comparison companies would have grown to $995, more than twice the general market. But your $1 in the visionary companies stock fund would have grown to $6,356 — over six times the comparison fund and over fifteen times the general market.'

Consider the impact of values in terms of value. Value, of course, is the most fundamental concept of economic transaction. Value itself is the result of a values-based process. The value added to or gained from a transaction is dependent on the values the parties perceive to be affected. To determine what value we attach to a product or service, we first need to evaluate the added benefit it provides us with. Each benefit is underwritten by a value — that is, a preference on how we would like something to be or not be — along with how important that outcome is to us. Values are the criteria for determining value. Our preferences and priorities (values) enable us to determine for ourselves the innate or instrumental worth of a product or service. Hence our evaluation of worth (value) is formed by our preferences or priorities assessment and is therefore values-based. In short, value is determined by what is important to you in a particular context.

Economics is based on perceived value, i.e. the ability, merit or benefit a product or service can provide to enhance our experience of our underlying values. Hampden-Turner and Trompenaars, authors of the book *The Seven Cultures of Capitalism*, say: 'Preferences, or values, are the invisible hands that regulate economic activity, and the source of economic strength or weakness.'

The interconnectedness between values and value seems blatantly obvious once it is pointed out. However, the relationship is easy to ignore or overlook. In *Cannibals with Forks*, John Elkington notes: 'The failure of economists to understand wealth creation flows from the fact they study how people use money, not why or what are their motives. Behind all economic transactions are people making choices based on their values.'

Underneath all economic transactions is an unstated measurement of human energy. Financial currency is nothing more than a convenient measurement and representation of human energy. Human energy is a physical, emotional, mental and spiritual expression of our underlying values. Anything we do, think or feel is based on values. We are compensated for our energy expenditure in business (i.e. working) by receiving payment for that work. The perceived value of our work effort and the perceived value of our pay are evaluated through the filters of how the organisation or job market prioritises skills and experience. An organisation that values work ethic, productivity, management and financial success will be getting value for money from an individual who displays these characteristics.

In simple terms, 'value for money' is determined by the degree of fulfilment of individuals' and businesses' values. Our values are what we put our energy into, and dollars are nothing more than a perceived measurement of that energy's worth. Money, in most respects, is spent only to increase the amount of energy we have or decrease the amount of energy we are expending. Although money itself is not a value, what it stands for and can provide us with most certainly are values.

Another measure of financial performance, shareholder returns, and its correlation with values alignment, was measured in an American study by Richard Barrett. Over a 10-year period, shareholders' return was 23 per cent in the 61 publicly held companies that make up the list of the 100 best companies to work for in America. This compared with 14 per cent over the same period with the average company on the general index of American Industry (Russell 3000 Index). For a company to be considered a 'best' company to work for, its values would have to align with those of its employees.

Growth

In *Corporate Culture and Performance*, Kotter and Heskett showed that values-based organisations, over an 11-year period, outperformed other organisations. Their growth was four times faster, job creation seven times higher, and stock prices grew 12 times faster; profitability was on average 750 times higher than non-values-based organisations.

This all makes for impressive reading, yet it doesn't take a genius to recognise that people are going to perform at a higher level if they enjoy their work, it is meaningful to them and they perceive that it is genuinely contributing to the overall fulfilment of being alive. All of these feelings are natural results of experiencing values alignment.

Intellectual capital

Intellectual capital can best be described as the difference between an organisation's book value and its market value. Intellectual capital is the key to know-how, innovation and doing it 'our way' and, as such, comprises a unique values set. This may include such values as achievement, adaptability/flexibility, communication/information, construction/new order, convivial technology, corporation/new order, creativity/ideation, and so on — see Appendix 2 for further examples. With the advent of corporate takeovers and globalisation, accountants are increasingly being asked by organisations to factor such information into the balance sheet. This has not always been the case; as Robert Jones points out in *The Big Idea*, 'Investors and analysts place value on what is rare. Tangibles — buildings, machinery, technology — are readily available. Capital is readily available. What is in short supply is the intangible.'

Values are intangible; they do not, however, have to be in short supply. To benefit from this intangible resource all organisations have to do is define their values and align to them.

Emotional capital

Emotional capital is also increasingly recognised as being as important to business as financial considerations. Emotional capital includes customer goodwill, visionary leadership, positive attitudes, employees' endeavours, willingness, passion, commitment and loyalty, all of which are values that fundamentally contribute to an organisation's success. Emotional capital is constantly on loan from the members of the organisation, suppliers and customers. If the organisation is not values-based it risks losing the use of the creativity, ideas, insight and understanding that come from emotional capital.

In some cases, the ability of organisations to benefit from staff's intellectual capital is obviously dependent on employees' willingness to share their creativity and knowledge. Our research has indicated that employees' willingness to work is directly related to values alignment with the company.

Aligned values increase staff morale

All the organisations that we have been involved with in supporting their efforts to become values-based have reported increased staff morale. This morale increase has sometimes resulted from some staff leaving (of their own choice) to work or engage in other activities considered to be more in alignment with their personal values. However, increased morale can mostly be attributed to people clarifying their own personal values and aligning them with their work.

Reduced corruption

An open culture that operates with shared values often relieves the need for covert, hostile behaviour such as corruption. Research in Holland by Gerard Endenburg, author of *The Sociocracy Method*, suggests that corruption occurs when there is some degree of separation between what is wanted and the ability of the individual to attain it. The Dutch police force has applied the shared values-based sociocracy model with great success, reducing corruption within the force. The process is based on defining and providing for people's highest priorities in a given situation. The Dutch government is now studying how the process can be applied elsewhere in its institutions and wider society.

While we were working with one organisation, an employee came forward as a result of having clarified his own personal values and admitted to having stolen stock from the company over the past six months. When asked why he had finally come forward and confessed, he answered, 'Well, believe it or not, honesty is one of my highest values. I guess I'd forgotten that until recently.'

Values enable faster reactions and decision-making

Values enable us to react faster by creating predetermined and aligned thought processes. They also create a common understanding that enables us to act coherently and effectively with minimal communication. Values are like the key words used in an Internet search — by knowing the words and applying them, we are able to simplify our search for understanding and also act more quickly.

Decision-making is improved because individuals need only refer to the company's values to determine the best course of action to achieve the desired results. Values underpin all our decisions, because choosing any option is always based on what we consider to be our preferred outcome or what is most important. Aligned and consistent decision-making in an organisation is an outcome of aligned values.

Grahame Maher, CEO of Vodafone Pacific, believes his senior management team are good at making decisions and gaining consensus because they work within the values framework of the organisation. 'People can now feel what is the most appropriate course of action. We don't have to stop and think it through. If it is aligned with our values, it feels right and we do it.'

This intuitive style of decision-making occurs because values are emotionally based and are therefore predominantly associated with the limbic system, a collection of unlinked structures in the brain that are particularly important in unconscious motivational and emotional behaviours. The prefrontal cortex (or neocortex) is the centre for the conscious processes of rational analysis and logical deduction. Because these conscious processes require mental manipulation, they occur more slowly than emotional responses. David Clutterbuck and Walter Goldsmith noted in their book, *The Winning Streak Mark 2*: 'People who are unfortunate enough to lose access to their limbic brain and have to rely on their neocortex prove unable to make even simple decisions. It seems that we need an overlay of emotional content to make rational judgements.'

Improved customer service and relationship-building

Values-based management includes clarification of what the organisation stands for and how its values support this. On understanding these values and the organisation's overall purpose, staff are better equipped to act conscientiously and independently to deliver service if — and only if — service is a value of the organisation. In organisations where service has been identified as a value, managers have reported increases in customer-service results because staff have been able to identify with their role more effectively.

Increased commitment by sales staff

We have seen phenomenal improvements in the sales performance in some organisations where we were asked to work specifically within the sales department. For example, after one day working with a sales team to clarify their core values, the team as a whole increased sales by a monthly average of 37 per cent.

When we reviewed the reasons for this increase, the salespeople unanimously reported that in clarifying the core values of their role, they provided themselves not only with a reason for doing the job, but also with a compelling reason to succeed. Many of the team reported things such as, 'It's given me huge motivation to get out there and be of service', 'I'm not afraid of selling any more', and 'I've got a passion for what I'm doing now'. Values underpin the integrity of your services and products.

What you stand for sells. Values enable who you are and what you stand for to become just as important as what you sell. Increasingly, marketing departments are tapping into this concept to keep pace with society's perception of what type of companies they wish to support.

Recruitment

Organisations hire predominantly on 'head and hands'; that is, on what people know, how smart they are, what information they bring by way of their qualifications and experience and what ideas they have, along with their skills and practical ability. They fire people predominantly on 'heart': for attitude, tardiness, procrastination, dishonesty, lack of empathy or caring, laziness, inability to develop relationships and so on.

Increasingly, companies are using values inventories as part of their selection process to take the so-called 'heart' factors into account. By using technology capable of scanning documents to define which values are included and represented by the written word, and the AVI process (described in detail in forthcoming chapters), the chances of successful recruitment can be improved. The prospective employee's values alignment with the company is taken into consideration during the recruitment process.

Values build brand

Values provide a cohesive identity for the business both internally and externally. Shared values create alignment, which in turn provides trust and commitment. Brand loyalty is, in one respect, long-term values alignment.

If an organisation brands itself — or wants to — it will benefit enormously from clarifying the values and culture that reflect that brand. David Walden, director of the Auckland advertising agency Whybins TBWA, comments that a brand without values lacks soul and therefore is not going to engage people.

Decreased absenteeism

Peter Leathley, human resources manager at Boise, said the values alignment process has had a noticeable impact on reducing absenteeism in his organisation. He suggested, after we had facilitated a nationwide delivery of workshops to enable all staff to clarify their personal values, that it stood to reason that someone who had a deeply held reason to be at work was more likely to actually be there than someone without such a reason. He also said people tended to become more accountable because when employees are aware of the organisation's values and how they complement their own, they can recognise when they have made a mistake or are out of alignment.

Increased tolerance

Values awareness almost always leads to greater tolerance of others. Throughout values programmes delivered for our clients we emphasise that values are not right or wrong, they are simply priorities and preferences. A number of managers have commented that they find their employees are more considerate of each other's opinions, even though they may not agree with them.

Staff bring more of themselves to work

People regularly comment that in a values-based culture they feel safer to be themselves. They feel more genuine and at ease in expressing how they feel. This contributes to an overall feeling of fulfilment in their work.

Values drive commitment

To be committed to do something, we must assign some type of meaning, importance or preference to an action. What you want is driven by how much you want it.

Values also create meaning because they reflect the underlying beliefs that tell us why something is important to us. In turn, meaning creates commitment — try feeling committed to something that has no meaning for you. To put this into perspective, Posner and Schmidt, in a 1993 study of 1059 managers from a variety of industries across the USA, found that the average employee level of commitment stands at 65 per cent. Personal values awareness has proven on average to increase commitment in organisations to 92 per cent, a significant increase. Regardless of how high commitment is already in your organisation, an increase of this magnitude has to be good for you.

Added performance indicators

Values provide organisations with leading performance indicators. The most common performance indicators, such as sales revenue and profit, are lagging indicators; they only tell us how we've done after we've done it. While these delayed indicators are useful, a more immediate picture of performance is gained by working with performance indicators which are values-based. For example, at Burger King, a manager is able to quickly measure any behaviour, interaction or environmental condition in a restaurant through the organisation's three values of pride, passion and performance. All facets of the restaurant can be considered to determine whether the people at Burger King can take pride in them (Is the floor clean? Is my uniform tidy?). In the same way, customer service and collegial support can be evaluated as a reflection of the value of passion. Any outcome or result can be considered as having a positive or negative impact on the third value, performance.

Define and strengthen company culture

No company will prosper for long without a stabilised functional culture. Values are the invisible threads of culture — when they are congruent they create 'connection'. All relationships — between one person and another, between the present and the future, between customer and product, a team and its goals, a leader and a vision — are strengthened by aligned values. Strong relationships have strongly aligned values. Because values focus our attention, they also lead to the alignment of our efforts, which in turn strengthens relationships.

When an organisation has a defined set of values that are embodied by all employees there is less need for managing and control.

CHAPTER 3

Why the time is right

The management focus for the years 2000 to 2010 will be about managing meaning, which of course requires an ongoing interest in values.

Paul Chippendale, Director, The Minessence Group

—

Global values shift

Increasing numbers of people the world over are placing greater emphasis on values and are asking themselves values-based questions, such as what is life all about? What am I supposed to be doing? Who am I beneath all this routine, stress and struggle to pay bills? What, if anything, is my purpose in life?

The increasing public interest in self-help, personal development and financial management books, workshops, talkback shows and personal-growth exercises is testament to people's growing desire to understand who they really are and express what they really want in their lives. Institutions such as government departments, corporations, learning institutes and some would argue even churches, appear to be at a loss to provide any real answers for those seeking some sense of meaning in their lives. This increasing interest in searching and discovering meaning in one's life suggests a significant values shift is under way among people in the developed world. In *The Big Idea*, Jones writes, 'The psychologists say that we're shifting from being *sustenance-driven* (looking for basic needs to be met) through being *outer-directed* (looking for esteem and status) to being *inner-directed* (looking for self-fulfilment)'.

Perhaps what is most significant about this values shift is not that it's taking place at all, as much as the speed at which it's happening. Paul Chippendale, co-author of *New Wisdom II*, writes, 'In one generation, our collective world-view as a civilisation has dramatically altered. This has led to a significant shift in people's values.'

He quotes an international values survey conducted in 1994 by the Compass Group, a US-based consulting firm, that found the top eight priorities for people in the workplace to be:

1. growth and development of individuals

2. management taking a long-term view

3. management caring about all stakeholders

4. social responsibility

5. democratic participation in the organisation

6. ecological values

7. spiritual values

8. employee ownership.

Source: Colins and Chippendale, *New Wisdom II*

Chippendale concludes, 'The disparity between the values people currently hold as a priority and the institutional materialistic values is creating a tension that will force organisations to either realign their values to today's values or perish.' It is the gradual impact of this disparity that has led to organisations beginning to take notice of the signs of values conflicts and, as a result, taking a serious interest in values alignment.

Traditionally the emphasis has been on ensuring employees accepted the company's values and then went about passionately delivering them. What companies have failed to take into account is that employees cannot buy into the company's values when they fail to see how those values directly relate to their own lives. What's the point in having company values if your own people can't or don't want to buy into them?

How is it that companies fail to make the connection between the organisation's values and those of their employees? Ironically, it is because of just that fact — their own values are so important to them that they are blinded from even considering that the values of their people have a role to play in the success of the organisation.

The Compass Group also found compelling evidence of just how large the gap has become between company values and those of the individual. The survey notes that 'internationally, greater than 40 per cent of people would prefer a different job in a different organisation'. The numbers are greater in Europe and the Pacific Basin, at 60 per cent. These numbers are hard to accept on first reading; however, our informal survey of approximately 2000 people, conducted between 1999 and 2000, suggests the figure may even be as high as 70 per cent in New Zealand. No wonder organisations often struggle to motivate their employees, when the work they do lacks meaning for them. This is understandable when many organisations are predominantly focused on financial success, and what people hold as important in life is often different.

Duane Elgin, a social scientist and director of the non-profit organisation Choosing Our Future, has examined some of the major surveys conducted over the past decade and reached some important conclusions. In Gail Bernice Holland's book, *A Call for Connection*, Elgin refers to a world values survey, which revealed that, 'despite the economic problems in many areas of the world, majorities in most of the twenty-four nations surveyed gave environmental protection a higher priority than economic growth'.

Again this clearly indicates that what is most important to people is fundamentally different to the concerns of organisations. It also suggests that organisations have a significant role to play in supporting their employees to experience work as a meaningful endeavour.

Consider the phenomenon of misaligned values. The table opposite indicates the nine most common areas of misalignment between company and personal values. Part Two of this book looks at these and other areas of values misalignment in depth. In the meantime, we can begin to understand specifically what employees want from an organisation and what the workplace typically provides.

The table clearly demonstrates the disparity between the two sets

What employees want	What the workplace provides
AN ORGANISATIONAL CULTURE THAT: • values learning • supports learning from failure • focuses on the long term	AN ORGANISATIONAL CULTURE THAT: • expects 'right answers' • penalises failure • focuses on the short term
A MANAGEMENT STYLE THAT: • promotes openness • cares for and supports individuals • encourages risk-taking	A MANAGEMENT STYLE THAT: • promotes secrecy • motivates through fear
AN ENVIRONMENT THAT: • nutures personal satisfaction • supports freedom to express feelings • promotes a desire to grow/create	AN ENVIRONMENT THAT: • assumes financial motivation • stifles expression of feelings • is driven by survival needs

Source: The Compass Group & The New Leaders, 1994
quoted in Chippendale and Colins, *New Wisdom II*

of values. What people want and what the workplace provides can be significantly different. Why?

What you value tends to direct what you think about, what you see (and what you don't see, or overlook) and what and how you think. Collectively, these core attention-directing values, along with their underlying beliefs and associated values, create a viewpoint from which we view and interpret the world. The values sets outlined in the chart above suggests that individuals have a world-view that is self-actualising. This means people are exploring their world and trying to establish meaning in their lives in an attempt to find their place in the world. People with this type of world-view are usually committed to learning and are willing to accept mistakes as part of the learning process. They long to grow and probably define 'success' as achieving their full potential. They are happy to support others and in return receive support in their quest to be authentic.

Meanwhile the typical organisation has a world-view that is committed to maintaining the status quo. It values controlling behaviour rather than motivating. It is focused on performance for fear of failure, rather than potential in search of success. The organisation probably defines success as 'not failing' and achieves this by averting bankruptcy or not losing market share. The consequences of these differing world-views mean that the organisation is committed to managers measuring employees for results, inadvertently (and sometimes even blatantly) creating a fear-driven environment to motivate people to do enough to keep the organisation away from financial peril.

People often refer to this type of organisation as paternal and patron-ising. Employees feel demotivated (despite management's attempts to motivate them through threats and incentives). This misalignment of values between people and the organisation creates what Chippendale describes as a 'tacit hostile culture'. This means that people feel resent-ment, frustration, bitterness and anxiety. However, because it is not safe for them to express this for fear of retribution or other perceived con-sequences, people bury their feelings and thoughts. They talk quietly, privately, secretly among themselves and with friends and family about their dissatisfaction. As a result people deliberately keep solutions and ideas to themselves as they resent sharing them with an organisation that doesn't respect or value them, or because they don't perceive any tangible advantage in adding value to the organisation.

People operating in these types of organisations no longer question, challenge, make suggestions, offer alternatives or even commit them-selves to delivering their best. In a culture such as this, the organisation drives its knowledge base and potentially even its intellectual capital underground, or worse still, out the door, as people leave in search of an organisation with a better values fit.

When we start a values-based programme with an organisation we warn them that the work we are about to commence is likely to lead to, on average, 10 per cent of their people concluding that their personal values are unaligned with those of the organisation and deciding to move on. Many organisations are shocked at this figure. Ten per cent is a significant proportion of their organisation, although on closer analysis we often find the organisation's percentage turnover is already higher than this. It's safe to assume that misaligned values are behind most of the resignations.

The values shift — what's happening?

Organisations failure to recognise the disparity between the company's values and those of their employees will only worsen as time passes. If organisations are struggling with values alignment now, then over the next five to 10 years they will find the struggle still greater, as the following data indicates.

For the past 12 years the Values Education Network has been surveying the value priorities of the Australian workforce. They have noticed a significant shift in value priorities between 1988 and 1998, indicating that world-views are changing. A comparison of the top values of people in the Australian workforce in 1988 and 1998 is shown in the table below. The values are listed in order of priority from highest to lowest. Definitions of the values can be found in Appendix 2.

The values shift in the Australian workforce, 1988–1998	
1988	*1998*
management	self-competence / confidence
collaboration / subsidiarity	relaxation
decision / initiation	being self
responsibility	decision / initiation
rights / respect	family / belonging
self-competence / confidence	life / self-actualisation
family / belonging	synergy
sharing / listening / trust	generosity / service
being self	loyalty / fidelity
	sharing / listening / trust

Source: Minessence Group

Some important conclusions and implications for management can be drawn from this values shift.

Interpreting the values shift

The top 10 values in 1988 indicate that people at that time viewed the 'world of work' as being about:

- effective management
- delegation
- productivity is achieved through taking responsibility for one's actions
- treating each other with respect
- having the competence and confidence to undertake one's allocated role.

The top 10 values in 1998 indicate the majority of people in the workplace no longer view the world of work this way — there has been a paradigm shift. The cluster of the top three values (i.e. self-competence/confidence, relaxation and being self) indicates that people now want to develop competencies that are relevant to who they are as a person (i.e. being self) and at their own pace (i.e. relaxation). This interpretation is reinforced by the presence of the value 'life/self-actualisation' in the top 10.

In summary, in 1988 people felt compelled to work in order to live as they desired — any work would do, so long as it generated the revenue necessary to create their desired lifestyle. In 1998 people are first looking at who they are as a person and then seeking to create a life around this, including meaningful work that supports who they are as a person. Values alignment between people's personal values and organisations has an important and effective role in achieving this.

The implications of values shifts for management

Values are people's unconscious motivators. In the workplace, effective managers tap into people's values as a way of increasing levels of self-motivation. Clearly, if some managers are operating from the belief that the majority of people still hold the same values priorities they held in 1988, they will not be effective in increasing motivation levels. To motivate people today, managers need to allow employees more flexibility in the hours they work, when they work and how they work. Gone are the days when people spend hours engaged in activities they do not enjoy.

British author Robert Jones echos similar sentiments. He quotes a survey conducted in 1998 by Gallup that indicates, '77 per cent of people felt that they had no material comforts missing from their lives. What we all want now is something that goes deeper. In the developed world, where there's lots of choice, people are starting to echo King Lear's cry "reason not the need".'

The pace of change

In modern society, where changes seem to occur almost instantly and with little warning, a new economic, technological, political, or societal breakthrough (or breakdown) can take place almost overnight. Values may therefore shift or evolve at a rate previously unknown.

An organisation that is not values-based will struggle to maintain its identity during a period of change. A values-based organisation will, however, have the benefit of an explicit set of values that enable it to manage change effectively.

Some of the management orientations that have changed over the last century are set out in the table on the next page, and we can see how these orientations became the values paradigm for the decade. We can also observe the effect such values filters had on the management focus of organisations, industries and even the economy as a whole. The table shows how historical events such as war, scientific and mechanical breakthroughs, business innovation, economic crises and booms have influenced these values shifts. Without an understanding of the values at work during times of change, organisations often struggle to adapt to, predict and survive global values shifts. Chippendale suggests that, to lead any group effectively, leadership style must be congruent with the values of the followers.

As human consciousness shifts, people adapt and change their own personal values to meet the priorities they face. In doing so they often outgrow their company's values, leading to greater dissatisfaction in the workplace. While it's easy for organisations to fail to recognise this values shift, they certainly won't fail to miss its consequences. The indications are already there that some organisations are positioning themselves as early adapters in the field of aligning values at work.

Shifts in business values

Key values	Period	Change in management orientation
Growth	Early 1800s	Massive organisations created as a result of a focus on growth.
Efficiency	Late 1800s	Scientific methods applied to management with a view to making organisations more efficient.
Engineering	1910s	Production, inward-looking. Customers taken for granted.
Finance	1920s	Expansion. Finance focus.
Accounting	1930s	Depression. Tight cost control.
Production	1940s	War. Production focus.
Sales	1950s	Sales. Sell as much as you can of what you have.
Marketing	1960s	Marketing. Design what people want and sell it.
Strategic wider planning	1970s	Look for the relationship of the company to the business environment and place the company properly in that environment.
Strategic management	1980s	Create management structures to think of the possible future of the business.
Entrepreneurship	mid-1980s	Belief creates reality. More about image than substance. Means justify the end.
Competing world-views: social ecology / economic rationalisation	1990s	Social ecology: vision of direction combined with concern about how organisational activities impact on people and the environment. Economic rationalism: competing in a global marketplace, letting the free market determine what should survive.
Principled management / managing meaning	2000s	Focusing on using science to identify underlying principles to inform organisational and managerial theory.

Source: Minessence Group

Keeping an eye on the early adapters

We are moving from a world of selling (establishing and satisfying the customer's needs) into a world of buying (where people select your organisation over others because it better matches or fulfills their values). To attract such people to your organisation with greater ease, in greater numbers and over longer periods of time requires the organisation to have a clearly defined set of values that your customer relates to, believes in and experiences every time they are in contact with you.

Whereas in the past an organisation might have relied on its brand values to influence and manipulate the market and sales process, the organisation itself and what it stands for is now a significant factor in purchasing decisions. Customers are no longer happy just buying your product, they want to simultaneously 'buy into' what your organisation stands for. This values emphasis is still in its relative infancy; however, the speed of change in modern business is so rapid that organisations who fail to pay attention may find themselves out of step with their employees and customer base. Ignoring values or dismissing them in relation to business is no longer a strategic option, yet many business leaders are failing to incorporate the values shift in their thinking.

John Elkington, author of *Cannibals With Forks*, discusses the nature of early adapters in relation to a number of changes in society and business. He theorises that we pay attention to the leading adapters in order to get an indication as to where we may all be heading in the future and how organisations can begin to prepare to adapt and benefit from such changes. He uses the following model to demonstrate how values shifts, driven initially by innovators and early adapters, move through the stages of early and late majority to the point where only a few laggards have yet to adopt them.

Elkington suggests that among the values likely to move up the S curve over the next few decades are responsible consumerism, business ethics, environmental justice and intergenerational rights. He also feels that there will be an underlying shift in values as organisations and consumers make significant values-based transitions as outlined in the table on page 53.

What is of particular interest to values consultants and those of us interested or involved in values research and education is the relatively

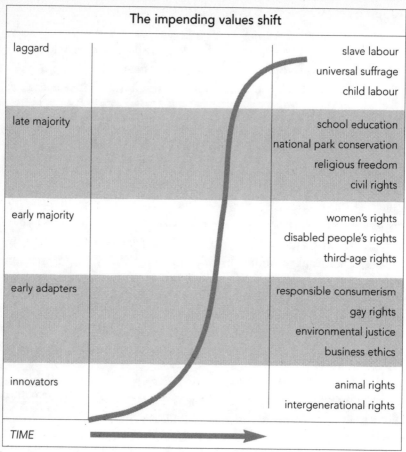

The impending values shift

laggard	slave labour
	universal suffrage
	child labour
late majority	school education
	national park conservation
	religious freedom
	civil rights
early majority	women's rights
	disabled people's rights
	third-age rights
early adapters	responsible consumerism
	gay rights
	environmental justice
	business ethics
innovators	animal rights
	intergenerational rights

TIME

Adapted with permission from John Elkington

slow pace at which leaders are able to identify these changes taking place within their own organisations, even among their own employees.

Elkington writes that as a result of this future values shift, 'The new agenda for business will increasingly revolve around values and ethics. Successful companies will be better at identifying, understanding, and responding to the values of those they work with and serve.'

Adapting to changing values

In *Lila: an inquiry into morals*, Phaedrus, the voice of Robert Persig's remarkable values odyssey, talks of trying to understand how to break into a culture and experience it; in other words, how to break into a different paradigm or values set.

Emerging Values		
Global Consumer *1990s*		*World Citizen* *2000s*
me	------------▶	we
more	------------▶	enough
materialism	------------▶	holism
quantity	------------▶	quality
greed	------------▶	need
short term	------------▶	long term
rights	------------▶	responsibilities

He discusses his experiences in an academic institution which, with its high levels of logic, was never going to accept anything other than its way of thinking. 'He called it the invisible wall of prejudice, a cultural immune system. But he also saw he wasn't going to get anywhere until that wall had been breached . . . The best he could do was mount a careful attack upon the wall . . . the key was values, he thought. That was the weakest spot in the wall of cultural immunity to new ideas.'

In order to avoid cultural immunity, organisations can easily begin to ingratiate themselves with their employees, markets and society by continually evaluating the values at work within them.

Consumers' values

Every organisation can easily identify what it sells. Very few, in our experience, successfully clarify and articulate what they stand for. One of the immense benefits of an organisation clarifying its values is that it identifies specifically what business it is in and why.

Because of the globalisation process, privatisation, education, information and competition, there are greater choices available to the consumer. People are in a better position than ever in the history of commerce to use their buying power to reflect their values. People are beginning to look a little more closely at the source of what is available to them.

Jones points out that there are dozens of websites that allow consumers to name the price they are willing to pay for products, from air tickets to cars, and the website finds the service or product. He notes 'suddenly it is the suppliers, not the buyers, who have to do the running around'.

As consumers we are increasingly hooked on using our purchases to reflect and identify who we are. Jones even suggests that political decisions, such as who we vote for, are influenced by who we perceive as most likely to spend government money (our taxes) in areas that best reflect our values. He suggests: 'As consumers seek to be the best they can be they are attracted to businesses that do the same.' We take into consideration as part of our purchasing criteria the reputation, philosophy and values of the organisations that produce our preferred and favoured products, as evaluated by our own personal values.

As we have seen, people are growing increasingly interested in self-actualising; learning to be themselves in as full a capacity as possible, mentally, emotionally, physically and spiritually. It appears that if organisations wish to optimise their opportunities in a market that is increasingly influenced by values, they need to consider an alternative marketing approach to those that many organisations currently operate with. 'It's about attracting people in, so that they can pull out the things they want,' says Roberts.

Consumers will, of course, continue to consider price and trends while making their purchasing decisions. However, they will also focus on the intangible aspects associated with their purchases as they increasingly consider these aspects of their own lives. Even money is becoming less 'tangible' as e-commerce, EFT-POS and online banking replace hard cash.

Customers are increasingly looking not just for value for money, they are also taking into account the concept of 'values for money.' Jones notes, 'People look for things they can identify with, the things they'd like to be part of, the things that make them feel better about themselves.' In this type of market, he suggests, 'Values matter most'. What your organisation stands for is becoming more important than what it sells.

Business consultant Dr Ian Brooks states in the opening words of his book *Second to None* that he has learned two things about business in the past 10 years: everyone believes their business is unique and everyone is wrong!

There is not a single organisation we have worked with that does not have a competitor offering a similar product or service at a comparable price. One way of differentiating your business from that of your competitors is by identifying, living and promoting your values. Not only is the market demanding this, it impossible for others to copy the way your organisation goes about living its core values. Jones rather poetically writes, 'Reacting against the blight of sameness, they're looking for distinctiveness. Awash with plenty, they're looking for rarity. Surrounded by the mass produced, they demand the hand made. With copies everywhere, they want the original. And with the population in most developed countries getting older, the cult of youth is starting to wane: more value will be attached to experience, less to novelty: more to reality, less to image. People are in search of authenticity.'

We advise organisations that sales is less about selling a product and more about informing consumers that your company conducts business in a way that most aligns with their values. In order to do this effectively, salespeople need to learn not only to identify the customer's needs, but to identify and relate to their values. The customer's needs only identify what the customer may want to purchase. Their values will show you how and why they wish to purchase, as well as indicating what other products they might consider purchasing.

Many salespeople respond positively to this concept because they don't like selling in the traditional way, finding it too pushy, manipulative, patronising, formulaic and unfulfilling. We have met very few sales-people who readily admit to having personal values that align naturally with those required to sell in the traditional way. Organisations that successfully adjust to the global shift in values and purchasing behaviours provide for themselves and their customers opportunities for long and prosperous relationships.

Jones reiterates this point: 'The demand then is for organisations to become the navigators: to cross the divide between seller and buyer, to put themselves on the consumer's side.' More organisations, in order to attract staff, investors, customers and suppliers, need to be clear about what their values are and communicate them successfully and convincingly (which includes living them) to all stakeholders.

These stakeholders will want to know what the organisation stands for above and beyond the obvious profitable returns. The organisation needs to consider whose values it wishes to align with and how it will go about achieving this as part of its performance strategy.

One of the most successful retail stores in New Zealand's commercial history, The Warehouse, sells practically everything you can think of. What it stands for is significantly more than that: it stands for everyone who buys from them getting a bargain and a money-back guarantee — and there are probably not too many New Zealanders who are unaware of this.

Misaligned organisations

Organisations that operate on values randomly or unconsciously or ignore their values altogether are referred to as 'misaligned organisations'. Such companies actually operate on values without knowing it. The organisation's values operate in a tacit manner within its structure and culture. Employees are driven to do things and achieve objectives without understanding the deeper meaning behind them. As the old maxim goes, 'giving someone a what without a why is training them in learned helplessness'.

In an unaligned organisation people operate by objectives and obligations rather than by preference. There is little or no awareness of the values that form the organisation's strategies. In an unaligned organisation, what it sells is by definition more important than what it stands for, because, by being unaware of its values, it is by definition unaware of what it stands for.

Up until relatively recent times, being a misaligned organisation probably didn't matter too much. Organisations had lots of managers to push employees along. However, the recent shift in values means that 'business as usual' will soon be a thing of the past. Any organisation that is aware of this values shift is making subtle changes within their organisations to begin to adjust to it.

Organisations that are doing this offer us a glimpse of the future of business. These organisations, led by visionary leaders, are doing everything in their power to understand this values shift, to adapt to it and join in. They are doing so for the benefit of their employees, their customers and society. These organisations are establishing themselves as a new type of enterprise. They are passionate about what they do. Their work is meaningful to them. They are clear about what they stand for. They genuinely care about their people. They insist on creating a work environment and culture that brings out the best in everyone. These organisations are aware of the impact of values on people, performance and profit. They work deliberately with values to create congruency between people's values and those of the organisation. They recognise the immense power of values and how they can be used to create meaning in their endeavours. They typically measure their success using a triple bottom line of financial, social and environmental accounting.

Organisations like this are the exception rather than the rule in today's business world and yet, given the world values shift, they are indicative of the future of organisations' cultural and strategic strength. In New Zealand, Vodafone and Burger King are prime examples of organisations committed to being values-based. There is a big difference between being committed to being values-based and claiming to be values-based. Many organisations claim to be values-based, yet in reality few actually demonstrate enough understanding of the values process to create a values-based culture.

Although every organisation's culture is different, and its values approach unique, there are techniques that can be successfully applied to all organisations seeking to become values-based. These techniques and the framework within which they can be implemented are set out in Part two of this book.

Implementing values in your organisation

What keeps me awake at night are the intangibles.
It's the intangibles that are the hardest thing for a
competitor to imitate. If we ever do lose that we
will have lost our most valuable competitive asset.

Herb Kelleher, CEO of Southwestern Airlines

—

CHAPTER 4

Overcoming management scepticism

Great people want to work at places where they can
actually use their talents, where they are treated with
dignity, trust, and respect, and where they are engaged
by the values and culture of the organisation.

Charles O'Reilly and Jeffrey Pfeffer, *Hidden Value*

—

Why do some managers need convincing?

On more than one occasion we have heard senior managers and business
leaders refer to values in business as 'irrelevant', 'the latest consultant
craze' or some 'new age, tree-hugging trip' — even a 'greenie conspiracy'.
Why would experienced, intelligent businesspeople have such a sceptical
and condescending reaction to the concept of values in business? After
numerous in-depth discussions with such managers, three key reasons
emerged to explain why they are so often dismissive of values.

1. Managers have experienced working with values previously and
   the experience was not successful.

2. Managers lack a clear understanding of what values actually are
   and how to work with them.

3. Managers are fearful of self-evaluation for personal or professional
   reasons.

Given these three statements, it's easy to see why managers could be reluctant to 'waste' time, effort and money on implementing a values programme. Before looking at how to resolve these situations we will examine each one in detail to better understand the issues involved.

Previous experience

The Management Agenda 2001 report (an annual survey conducted by Roffey Park in the UK) questioned 204 managers on issues affecting their work and wellbeing. According to the report, scepticism surrounding organisational values was high. Over 70 per cent of the managers surveyed said the organisation had espoused values. However, 60 per cent also said the espoused values of the organisation did not match the actual values of the organisation. Nearly 30 per cent said there was no incentive to practise the values, and 20 per cent also claimed the rewards systems of the organisation contradicted the organisation's values. Our experience in New Zealand and Australia suggests a similar situation exists here.

Lack of understanding

Many managers we have worked with confused values with emotions, morals, ethics, principles and even virtues. In doing so, they understandably struggled to see how values could possibly relate to their organisations in the first place. They also had little understanding of how values influence organisational culture. Usually, this isn't their fault, as very little attention is placed on the effects of values and their role within organisations in most management or business training. Many courses at universities offer little more than one lecture on the topic, or refer to it in passing as a part of their review of organisational cultures.

Within organisations themselves there is usually no training or education available on the topic at all. We are often invited to sit in on senior leadership teams' retreats to help them clarify their organisation's values. We observe the initial proceedings and frequently find that the team launches into haphazardly listing words they believe make suitable company values. At this point, we interrupt the proceedings to ask them to define what they mean by values, only to find that the team is unable to do this. This lack of understanding makes most attempts at creating values for an organisation redundant before the process has really begun.

Reluctance to be evaluated

Managers in today's frantic and competitive business environments find themselves under incredible pressure, mentally, emotionally and physically. However, if they work in a traditional environment, where emphasis is on an analytical and competitive approach to the job, managers may be afraid of evaluation, for fear of being found wanting in key areas, e.g. not coping with stress, having poor motivation or displaying an inappropriate attitude. The traditional hard-line approach of many organisations means it is still considered unsafe or foolish to communicate that you feel overwhelmed. Managers we have spoken with have confided that if they admit such 'frailties' they fear their reputations will be affected or they will be overlooked for promotions or participation in key projects. To protect themselves from such revelations they adopt a 'red badge of courage' approach and soldier on, often at enormous expense to their health, relationships and mental wellbeing. Such managers also express reluctance to engage in any evaluative process that could uncover these issues, especially something as thought provoking and revealing as understanding their own values and the influences these have on their leadership style. A number of managers admitted they do not even feel comfortable considering their own feelings and emotions, let alone sharing them with others. When invited to elaborate further on the reasoning behind this, male managers, in particular, commented that they considered expressing and discussing feelings in the workplace was not only inappropriate but also unprofessional and even immature.

It appears that over time, organisations have come to prize the dedicated worker who shuts out all personal feelings from their work. It seems there are still some organisations that pride themselves on the fact they can convert people into robot-like machines, capable of being switched on and released, to work dutifully without being inhibited by feeling emotions such as fear, anxiety or empathy. Many organisations seem to have conditioned people to believe that work is a contradiction to meaning, fulfilment and emotion. This dehumanising of the work environment is one of the major reasons why so many people don't want to work in the type of companies and roles they are currently in.

'We don't want people bringing their emotions to work.' A manager once said this in response to a comment made in a presentation to his organisation about the benefits of encouraging people to bring their deepest-held values to work. We asked him if he had told his team that. 'Absolutely,' he said. 'We're here to do a job, not run a therapy clinic.'

How happy would he be if none of his people brought to work things such as commitment, loyalty, motivation, caring, empathy and honesty? All of these attributes are driven by emotions and are based on values. When we asked him about this he looked a little confused and said, 'Well, I didn't mean that, of course.' After a pause he frowned and said, 'Mind you, I am not sure I've explained that to my team. I always say work and emotions don't mix.' He concluded by saying, 'I'll have to clarify that with them in my next team meeting.'

Later in a private conversation, the manager said he had truly not recognised that there are emotions that it is very useful for people to demonstrate at work. He was simply doing what he had always been told by his own managers.

We suggested the manager adopt the phrase: 'Free to enthuse!', meaning that organisations would do well to support their managers and staff to free themselves of any limitations, whether beliefs, habits, attitudes or circumstances, so they are enthused about their work. We continued with a lively and interesting discussion about what it takes to free people from their own preoccupations while leaving them enthusiastic about the work required from them. We discussed such topics as on-the-job coaching, mentoring, health and safety training, and by the end of the conversation the manager was even suggesting the organisation should help employees with career counselling if the employee wished to take advantage of such support.

Companies pay for people's time, physical presence and brain power to perform from nine to five, five days a week (and sometimes much longer); yet the things they can't buy, things that will only be given if the circumstances are right, such as passion, commitment and loyalty, could be so readily available if only the company made it safe for the individual to bring their whole selves to work. As Napoleon once said, 'You cannot buy a man's life, but he will give it to you for a medal.' Creating a 'suppressed emotions' culture at work guarantees the misalignment of people's values with those of the company. If anything, we need to shift the paradigm to 'Bring your deepest values and emotions to work — your organisation needs them!'

How to handle management scepticism

Provide education sessions on the nature of values and their benefits to business

Develop information sessions using the following chapters as guidelines. For example, to introduce the concept of values, managers could identify what they consider the preferred way of operating within their departments. They could then identify the words and their meanings (outlined in Appendix 2) that best represent those priorities. When they have completed this, explain that the words they have selected are in fact values.

We have often found that showing people how their day-to-day tasks are in fact values reduces scepticism dramatically. For example, the table below shows a daily diary and the values associated with the scheduled tasks.

	Tasks	Associated values
8 am	Drop kids at school	Family / Belonging
9 am	Prepare budget	Economic / Success
		Efficiency / Planning
11 am	Catch up on emails	Communication / Information
12 pm	Lunch	Function / Physical
2 pm	Team briefing	Communication / Information
		Evaluation / Self-System

Explain the relationship between people, values and systems

In order for managers to understand how values influence their business, we often say that all organisations comprise three fundamental components: people, values and systems. These three components form a loop in which feedback is circulated about quality, direction, capability, intention, progress, alignment and other critical performance indicators. chapter 11 explores this in more detail.

This viewpoint enables us to see business as a set of priorities and preferences (*values*) set by *people* to be achieved, measured and refined using various *systems* (technology, procedures and knowledge).

Viewing a business in this manner makes it easy to see how and where values fit in. Values are the framework for connecting people to the systems.

The Nature of Values in Organisations

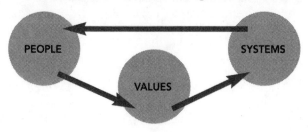

Involve managers in a simple evaluation of their business as a values-based organisation

Whenever we are involved in supporting an organisation to become values-based, we inevitably start, just as we have done in this book, by making sure those involved know exactly what working with values entails. This usually includes showing the leadership teams what the end result or final outcome of creating a values-based organisation looks like.

The following points are the key distinguishing traits or factors we have identified as defining a values-based organisation. These points have been drawn from our research and experience working with organisations, along with client feedback about what has worked; they also take into consideration overseas research and case studies. The list is not conclusive, as each organisation will inevitably have its own unique variations depending on its culture, values make-up and operating conditions.

To find out how explicit your organisation's values are, give yourself one point for each yes answer to the following 21 statements.

1. Your organisation stands for something more than just making a profit and increasing shareholder returns. Profit is seen as a means to an end.

2. Your organisation is clear about what business it is in. Everyone in your organisation knows what the company stands for.

3. Your organisation has a clear values set that is based in reality and is deliverable.

4. Your organisation's values are consistent and aligned with the organisation's vision.

5. Your organisation's values include both those that have

consistently contributed to the success of the organisation in the past and those that will add value to it in the future.

6. Your values are defined and, if necessary, prioritised in a hierarchical format.

7. Your values are aligned with and supported by the beliefs in your culture.

8. People know how to personally express the values in thoughts, words and action. Your staff consider themselves custodians of the company's values, rather than just recipients.

9. All people in your organisation have been provided with the opportunity to understand their own personal values and determine to what extent they are aligned with those of the organisation.

10. Your organisation's values are linked to the organisation's capabilities.

11. Your leaders are aligned with and champion the company values.

12. Your organisation recruits to its values and your induction programmes include an orientation of your organisation's values.

13. Your values are consistently represented in all internal and external communication.

14. Your values are used to create performance guidelines that are in turn used to inspire and measure performance.

15. Values-based thinking dominates your organisation.

16. Your values form the basis for all decision-making.

17. Your values create and enhance loyalty and understanding.

18. Your employees feel they are making a difference in their work. Their jobs are meaningful to them.

19. Your values contribute to a 'we'-oriented company culture and experience.

20. Your values add value to your customers' experience.

21. Your employees are clear about where and when you want the values applied.

Count how many of the 21 points you answered 'yes' to, then put a cross in the appropriately numbered box in the chart below.

Misaligned   Aligned

1	2	3	4	5	6	7	8	9	10	11	12	13	14	15	16	17	18	19	20	21

◄ Tacit values culture   Explicit values culture ►

Any score to the left of number 11 means your organisation tends towards misalignment and suggests that the values within your organisation are predominantly tacit (hidden and unknown). Any score to the right indicates a more aligned values-based organisation. This in turn suggests a more explicit and deliberate expression of your company's values.

Enable managers to clarify their own personal values

When managers understand their own values and the influence of these on their management style, preferred thinking strategy and world-view, they are better able to understand how values impact on the company's performance.

Recommend books

Books that explain the benefits of introducing a values-based culture to an organisation will help managers to understand these concepts. *Built to Last* by Collins and Porras has proven to be very popular with a number of our clients but there are many other books available, a number of which are listed in the bibliography.

CHAPTER 5

The strategic importance of values

Strategic values, the way most
organisations do them, are neither.

Robert Fritz

—

Values in organisations are usually not considered or adopted with a strategic emphasis. Most organisations do not, for example, consider relating their values to their vision or mission statement, or even understand the importance of doing so. Typically, the creation of a values set is no more than a list of aspirations the company wishes would happen in reality. The values are created without reference to the organisation's vision or its reason for existing.

Furthermore, organisations tend to place a greater emphasis on creating a vision than they do on developing a set of values, as the vision is more logically appealing. It's useful to have a vision, as it provides everyone with a chance to see where the company is going and what is its overall goal. Having a vision makes sense. Values, on the other hand, are rarely understood in terms of what they mean, how they work, where they fit and what benefits they provide. Often companies only resort to developing a set of values because 'everyone else is doing it', 'it's good for morale', 'it's great P.R.', or it is perceived as 'the hallmark of other successful organisations'.

This emphasis on vision over values is a little ironic as a vision actually comprises a set of aspirational values, i.e. a set of values that the organisation wishes to experience in the future. These aspirational values (the vision) are often referred to by values consultants as 'goal values'. However, a vision is of little or no use without 'means values' — values we must embody in order to achieve our goal values. When a vision exists without a set of means values it is equivalent to an Olympic athlete who dreams of winning a medal, yet has not placed any priority on preparation or training.

Visions have come under close scrutiny from management and strategic experts. Peter Senge, author of *The Fifth Discipline*, suggests a vision is often too abstract for people to relate to in the context of their particular job, or is seen as being too far removed in terms of the time it will take to achieve. He suggests that the vision is often so far in the future that people presume they will no longer be with the organisation by the time it is achieved.

Our own work with individual's values within organisations suggests that often the company vision is perceived to have nothing to do with the individual, who can see no personal benefit from achieving the vision. This often happens when a vision is predominately focused on maximising shareholders' returns or being number one in the market (great for shareholders, although not necessarily for any other type of stakeholder).

The human resources manager of a leading New Zealand food manufacturing company commented in a recent meeting, 'Not so long ago a vision could look out five or 10 years or even longer into the future. Now, because of the speed of changing priorities, and with the impact of innovations, a vision might only look ahead five to six months.' The speed of innovation in technology, knowledge and information affects many organisations. Their vision might change several times within the space of two years. Such a situation was almost unthinkable as little as five years ago. Company values, however, if effectively determined, remain the same.

Heather Leslie Swan, a leading Australian values consultant and executive coach, commented that from her experience working with CEOs all over the world, the values of an organisation were far more important to the company than its vision. 'The values operate and impact on the business — you live with them on a daily basis. The vision is in the future. If you live the right values, you'll get to the vision.'

Swan's comments touch on one of the most important aspects of the strategic use of values within organisations. When implemented in this manner an organisation's values provide a solid foundation for consistency around which the organisation can continually orient itself. Senge writes, 'Values are necessary to help people with day-to-day decision-making. Purpose is abstract. Vision is long-term. People need guiding starts to navigate and make decisions day to day.'

Understanding the relationship between values, vision, mission and strategy

A strategy is a plan to move in a chosen direction. Imagine that a company's vision is to sit on top of a wall. It's been decided that a ladder is the most effective way of achieving that goal. The choice of a ladder and the method of climbing the ladder can be seen as representing the organisation's strategy.

The ladder consists of rungs and side railings into which the rungs or steps are set. The rungs represent the critical success factors, competencies or objectives the company has to achieve if they are to scale the

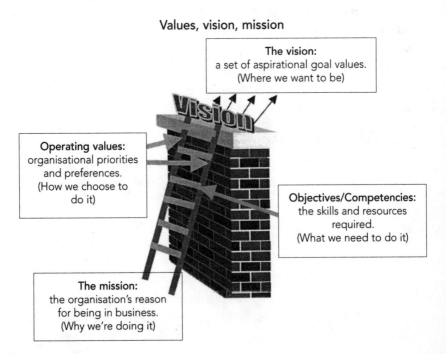

Values, vision, mission

The vision:
a set of aspirational goal values.
(Where we want to be)

Operating values:
organisational priorities
and preferences.
(How we choose to
do it)

Objectives/Competencies:
the skills and resources
required.
(What we need to do it)

The mission:
the organisation's reason
for being in business.
(Why we're doing it)

ladder and reach the top of the wall. The side railing represents the values or operating parameters of the business. Values form the operational and cultural guidelines within which the company performs.

The trick then is for organisations to define their values, and then develop strategies, systems and capabilities that support their values. The values in turn support the organisation to achieve its vision. For values to be considered strategic they need to be aligned with the vision and mission of the organisation.

How to evaluate your vision and mission in relation to your values

If you were living the values you created for your organisation in every facet of the business, would this lead to the achievement of your organisation's vision? Before you can answer this question, you may have to develop specific meanings or behaviour guidelines for each of your values first, in order to effectively determine exactly what living the value would mean.

Now, if you were living these same values, would they lead you to achieve your company mission?

Finally, ask yourself, whether by achieving your mission and vision, would the end result of both honour your values?

As a result of considering these questions you find that there isn't a complementary fit between the organisation's vision, mission and values, it could mean one of several things:

1. You may have the wrong values to achieve the vision.

2. You may have a mismatch between your vision and mission, and your values.

3. You may have to link the vision with the values of your emloyees.

You may have the wrong values to achieve this vision

You may have identified that in living your values, you will not achieve your vision or mission, because the values do not lead you in that direction. This could be because your values are not defined explicitly or fully enough, in terms of meaning and behaviour. It could also be that you have selected inappropriate values for achieving the vision.

Consider whether the values your organisation has selected are going to help the organisation to achieve its vision. If the answer is 'no', consider whether it's the vision or the values (or both) that need to change.

If you do not have any acknowledged organisational values read through the next few chapters to learn how to develop some.

You may have a mismatch between your vision and mission, and your values

Often, values feel non-negotiable, while the vision and mission feel out of sorts. The values appear more important than the organisation's vision or the mission. If this is the case, consider rewriting the vision and mission to represent a more fitting expression of your organisational values.

Alternatively you may have decided that the vision was in fact likely to change at some time in the future, perhaps due to the changing nature of the industry, yet the values would still be relevant in a hundred years. You might even drop your vision altogether or express it simply as, 'Our vision is to fully live our values!'

You may have to link the vision with the values of your employees

Remember that organisations do not live their values, people do. Likewise, no strategy is effective without the committed support of the organisation's people.

A vision statement describing a compelling future is typically only of benefit to a minority group, such as the shareholders and the current leadership team. This makes it difficult for an employee to arrive at work every day and deliver their best efforts towards achieving the vision. Too often employees feel that their company's vision has nothing to do with them or their lives.

A meaningful vision is one that encapsulates a 'common wealth'. In other words, any employee reading it would be inspired and want to be involved in achieving it in some way. This may even apply to a customer, investor or supplier. Imagine having a vision that inspired all stakeholders to get behind you and assist you in its manifestation. Imagine if people read your vision statement and thought, 'What an amazing organisation this must be. I would love to work for an organisation like this. I must remember to use their services from now on. I didn't realise this is what they stood for.'

Do your company's vision and mission statements have this effect on people? Or do they simply state that you want to be the best in your field, delivering service above your customers' expectations and providing your shareholders with a return on their investment?

Remember that people need meaning. The more meaning you provide, the more they will contribute. Imagine if your organisation represented more to its people than just being a company to work for. Instead, what if what your organisation stood for, its mission and values, were so inspiring and uplifting to your employees that it made them feel that their work was meaningful. Imagine the effect on morale, recruitment, absenteeism, corruption, silent sabotage and the like.

How do your company vision and mission statements stack up? Are they inspiring and meaningful to all who read them?

In summary, the process of reviewing your vision, mission, strategies and values can be represented graphically as shown opposite. The order of steps may change if the company is a start-up; however most companies we work with have existing vision, mission and strategies in place, and need to ensure they are consistent with their values.

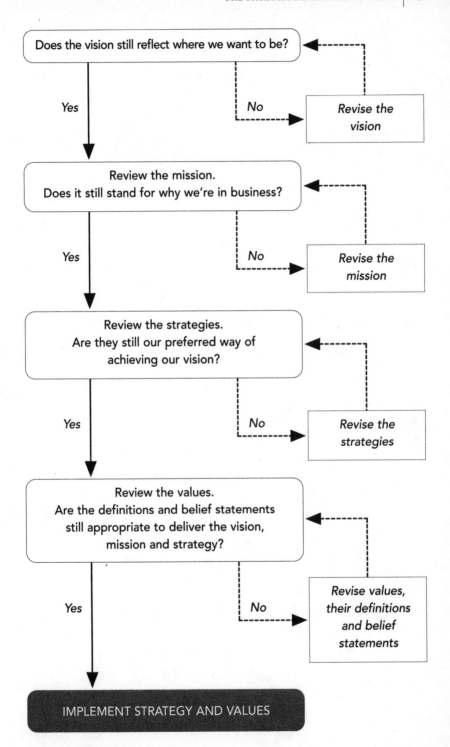

CHAPTER 6

Introducing values alignment

The Swedish word for business is 'naringslivet',
which means nourishment for life.

Getting people to pay lip service to company values is one thing, getting them to 'own' the values is quite another. Many organisations do not make this distinction and consequently get the whole values initiative wrong. When people care about their organisation, they become the organisation. Alignment between the company's values and employees' values is the real key to any organisation succeeding in genuinely living and experiencing its values.

Paul Chippendale suggests that organisational cultures can create a cultural system which is 'immune' to its own people. This immunity can disempower people in four ways: by subordination, emulation, mystification and contamination.

Subordination

In subordination, the organisation's values are presented as being 'higher' values than people's personal values. Chippendale offers author Rita Liljestrom's thoughts as an example: 'What does it do to treat women and men alike if the whole system is permeated by a male culture? If all society's prioritised values rest on a collective male consciousness, then what is equality but assimilation in the dominant culture?'

We see this often in business where women have to subordinate the more feminine values of their personal preferences (e.g. synergy) to the more masculine values of the overall organisation (e.g. performance) in order to achieve their potential within the organisation.

Emulation

In emulation, the organisation requires people to act the 'right' way in front of those who matter. This is often experienced in a culture of fear, leaving people open to manipulation in a variety of forms. Emulation occurs frequently within organisations that insist people deliver the organisation's values through their job description, resulting in people saying and performing only what is expected of them.

On the surface this culture appears to be values-based, as people are seen to be living the organisation's values. However, the organisation then falls into the trap of believing the values it observes in action are genuinely the organisation's values. The underlying suppressed values the people have an even higher preference for are not noticed.

This was powerfully shown in Afghanistan the day after the fall of the Taleban. Practices that had previously been banned appeared on the street within 12 hours: prohibited music, colourful clothes, soccer balls and unveiled women. The real values of the people had not been genuinely aligned with those of the ruling power and emerged the instant it was safe to do so. The people had simply emulated the values that were expected because of fear of the consequences.

Mystification

Mystification is the process of confusing those whose values you oppose into thinking they believe in your own values. We have witnessed this in high-performance sales cultures where sales representatives are confused into believing that their values are profit, competition and productivity, when in reality they may value family, recreation and relaxation more highly. This is achieved through overt or covert manipulation.

Contamination

Contamination occurs when the organisation's values are presented and perceived as being the ideal way of achieving your personal values. For example, a sales representative might begin to believe that success in sales (the organisation's value) leads to enhanced experience of their personal values of family, recreation and relaxation.

Values alignment

To avoid these types of disempowering cultures arising within an organisation, it is necessary to achieve a high degree of alignment between the values of the employees and those of the organisation.

Alignment occurs when the organisation's values and those of the individual are complementary. They do not have to be exactly the same, they simply have to support one another. If you have ever experienced driving a car with misaligned wheels, you are aware of what it feels like to operate when things are out of alignment, steering needs to be continually corrected, wheels wobble, the axle is put under excessive strain. Organisations experience similar disfunction when there is misalignment between their values and the values of the employees.

The effects of aligned or unaligned activity within a company can be observed in as short a period as six months. Chippendale says, 'When there is a match between the core personal values of most people in the organisation and core organisational values, the scene is set for personal fulfilment and organisational success. The conditions for optimal productivity are also set. In most cases, increased profitability follows.'

There appear to be some common factors that indicate low or nonexistent values alignment, resulting in lost business opportunities in sales and unproductive results in production and distribution. The table opposite lists some typical factors that occur when some degree of values misalignment is present in an organisation.

Until an organisation's values are aligned with those of its employees, there is little chance of operating at optimum efficiency. There is plenty of talk in today's business world about people being the company's greatest asset, yet few organisations actually practise what they preach. Fortunately things seem to be changing and companies are realising that when people are aligned with the organisation's values there are noticeable improvements to be gained. The table on page 80 highlights some of these areas.

The alignment of individual and company values is critical to sustaining corporate success. Behind every business activity and transaction are people making decisions based on their values; some activities are given high priority, others low priority. The number of aligned decisions being made by management and individuals on the company's behalf

Misalignment of Values	
Experienced by the individual	*Experienced by the company*
lack of commitment and attentiveness	high turnover in staff
feeling obliged not passionate	burned-out, fatigued employees
silent sabotage through lack of caring	procrastination
stress, lethargy, apathy	lowered productivity/profit
mistakes and placing blame	customer complaints
low job satisfaction	low staff morale
low productivity	authoritarian leadership, incentive-dependent employees
increase in need/desire for sick leave	low accountability/performance issues
discreet job searching during work hours	less recruitment appeal
self-imposed limitations	increased absenteeism
less creative input and problem-solving	communication breakdown

directly impacts on the overall strategic success of the company. Given that alignment is the key to success, it is essential to establish the extent to which your people are aligned with your company's values. Imagine the time, productivity and wastage — the cost in dollars — every time a person makes a decision based on value preferences that are not in line with the values of your company.

Our research shows that organisations that create values alignment improve their performance in terms of being more productive, more focused, and better places to work and to deal with.

Aligned values lead to aligned performance. For example, a sales culture that is aligned will have people engaged in the sales process who love what they do, and are committed to doing it well.

Alignment of staff and organisational values

Value	Benefit
Productivity	People are focused through the organisation's values
Profitability	People who are aligned with the values care about results
Vision alignment	The vision becomes a reality through the living of the values
Team culture	People committed to a common set of values strengthen culture
Passion	Aligned values create synergy and unleash passion
Empowerment	Values empower people to make successful decisions
Commitment	People are always committed most to what they value most
Innovation	Aligned values can lead to the flow of ideas and solutions
Energy	Aligned values generate a positive sustainable flow of energy
Joy at work	People love to do work that is aligned with their personal values
Success consciousness	People focus on the successful and congruent delivery of values
Motivation	People are motivated when they can openly apply their personal values at work
Consistency	Consistency is achieved when priorities are clear and shared
Parameters	Values tell people to what they can say 'yes' or 'no'
Aligned decisions	Everyone makes decisions based on the same values

A misaligned sales culture, on the other hand, will find its sales people fearful and even resentful of the sales process. They will often have increased stress levels, will procrastinate, experience call reluctance and be more likely to misinterpret client objections.

Research by other authors

Other authors also touch on the significance of values alignment. Charles O'Reilly and Jeffrey Pfeffer, authors of *Hidden Value*, examine successful organisations that have achieved not only exceptional financial success, but have also become organisations that people want to work for and commit to. They suggest that these organisations have created something that even their most determined competitors cannot copy. This hidden value, they suggest, is not scarce or unique, but can be found in all organisations. 'It resides in the intellectual and emotional capital of the firm and is in the power of the minds and hearts of its people.'

They consider the differentiating factor that distinguishes these organisations from their competitors: 'Each of these organisations is based on a set of values that energise their people and unleash the intellectual capital potentially available in all organisations . . . Each of the firms has a well-defined strategy that helps it make decisions about how and where to compete. But these strategic decisions are secondary to living a set of values and creating alignment between values and people.'

Stephen Covey, in *The Seven Habits of Highly Effective People*, also acknowledges the importance of the relationship between the individual and organisation. 'In a very real sense there is no such thing as organisational behaviour, there is only individual behaviour. Everything else flows from that.' The degree to which organisations are able to support their people to align with the company's values influences enormously the overall outcome.

Richard Barrett, the former values co-ordinator of the World Bank notes in *Liberating the Corporate Soul*, 'The highest levels of commitment are achieved by satisfying our mental and spiritual needs. The greatest gift you can give an employee is the opportunity to become all they can become personally and professionally. Creating a company culture that aligns with the values of employees and society is the critical issue for business in the 21st century.'

It appears business success will increasingly depend on a strong sense of values and purpose within companies, and on the congruent delivery of these values with all stakeholders. Achieving this will take a lot more than human-resource people creating a list of values they would like employees to believe in.

How to create and identify values alignment

In many respects creating values alignment is the overall outcome of a comprehensive and successfully managed values programme, which by definition is dependent on a number of factors having been achieved. These include:

- The organisation's values have been determined and prioritised, and aligned with the organisation's vision and purpose.

- The values have been communicated to all staff, and people have been provided the opportunity to align their beliefs with the values.

- The values have been linked directly to the desired behaviours suitable for each role.

- People have been provided the opportunity to clarify and learn how the values are to be represented through their role.

- Coaching has been provided by managers to support staff to implement the values in their roles.

- All people recruited into the organisation have received a comprehensive values-based induction into the organisation.

- The organisation has a process to measure and audit the degree of values alignment it is able to sustain.

Each of these points is covered separately later in the book. However, it is worth emphasising here that a significant part of the alignment process is looking for and overcoming any constraints or obstacles that emerge within the culture that prevent the values being able to thrive.

The importance of this is twofold. Firstly, it enables the organisation to achieve values alignment more rapidly than if the constraints were left unnoticed or at least unaddressed. Secondly, this approach to values immediately shifts the emphasis of the culture to one of learning and correcting rather than one of fearing mistakes and covert behaviour.

Values misalignment

There are, of course, numerous indications of some form of values misalignment, the most common of which are listed in the following table. However, the best way to determine if behaviour is out of alignment (either your own or someone else's) is to notice if it just doesn't feel right. This may not sound like a particularly scientific approach, and it isn't; yet when management of any organisation has made significant progress on embodying their values they inevitably tell you that, intuitively, they just know when something is misaligned.

The overall impression that you get from an organisation that is not values-based is that it has no definable sense of purpose other than keeping people busy making money. Not that there is anything wrong with this, but this sole focus may not be the most beneficial for the company.

The organisation's culture lacks consistency as the various forces — whether economic, political, social or structural — pull it first in one direction before the opposing force pulls it back again. Until priorities are set and a strategy is implemented, this process continues.

As Robert Fritz, author of *The Path of Least Resistance for Managers*, notes, the values that dominate the organisation will displace other competing lesser values. Companies that are not values-based tend to have cultures dominated by the haphazard.

To be really confident of a high degree of values alignment, conducting an audit will determine the extent to which the values are assimilated into the business. This is the most effective way of gaining a deeper understanding of the values at work and their influence in an organisation. Information on values audits can be found in chapter 17.

Some common indications of values misalignment

Values misalignment indicators	Values alignment indicators
The leadership team shows no interest or alignment with the values.	The leadership team demonstrates the values in everything they do.
The business strategy contradicts the values.	The business strategy is based on its values.
The organisation recruits out of fear and needs.	The organisation recruits to its values.
Values are talked of as being soft, new age or irrelevant to the business.	The values are taken seriously by people. They recognise and practise them.
Decision-making is not aligned with the values.	Values are the basis for all decision-making.
The values of the organisation are not known, not understood or ignored.	The values, their meaning, and application are understood by all.
The organisation's performance oscillates.	The organisation advances towards its vision.
A tacit culture pervades the organisation. Knowledge and information are hidden and withheld.	The values create a sense of belonging and an explicit culture promoting a sense of 'we'.
People are only here to earn a wage.	People feel they make a difference. Their work is meaningful.
People are loyal to themselves.	People are loyal to the organisation.
Incentives are necessary to enhance performance.	Values alignment creates and inspires potential.
People in the organisation do not appear to know their personal values.	All people within the organisation know their personal values and are aligned with those of the company.
Customers do not receive value for money.	Customers experience 'values for money' and receive value for money.

CHAPTER 7

How to create values alignment

If you're not aligned, you can't walk the talk.

—

Many leaders have a limited awareness of the importance of their organisation's values. One conversation we had with a CEO is typical — when asked about the work in her company that had been done with values, she responded, 'Values, yeah we did all that two years ago, that's them on the wall over there.'

As the conversation progressed it became very apparent that she was convinced that having a list of values articulated on her office wall meant they were alive and well within the business. Many leaders make the same oversight.

After the release of *Built to Last* by Collins and Porras, leadership teams the world over headed off to strategic retreat sessions to identify their core purpose and define, discover or create their core values. The benefits of doing so as outlined in *Built to Last* were compelling. Organisations could expect to improve performance, lift share value, attain greater growth, and most impressively, create sustainable leadership within their market. The only problem was that many of these leadership teams knew next to nothing about the context, nature and structure of values.

Those charged with creating the organisation's values often confused values with the likes of morals, ethics and emotions, as well as totally ignoring the role beliefs play in the effective and successful creation of meaningful values sets. The end result? Often little more than lip service to a set of 'values' that were quickly put aside, ignored or scoffed at as people busied themselves with business as usual.

Many of the managers charged with creating their organisation's values lacked any knowledge or understanding of 'cultural structure'. This is not surprising given that education in the finer points of cultural anthropology is not a key feature of most business education programmes. It's a great pity — even a rudimentary overview of some of the anthropological and psychological models created to define and understand culture would help people to better understand the role of values in organisations.

Failure to understand where values fit in an organisation's structure and culture is a significant factor in the inability of so many organisations to live their values successfully.

The good news is that the anthropological models are simple, quick to interpret, proven and easy to apply. One of the key models is that of Robert Dilts, a pioneer and expert in the field of neurolinguistic programming. Dilts suggests that an organisation is the result of the interaction of what he refers to as its 'logical levels'. Each logical level, although clearly defined as an entity in itself, is dependent on and influences all other levels. The following section examines Dilts' model in more detail.

Values and organisational culture

Understanding structure

Dilts identified a number of logical levels that typically define an organisation's culture and leadership. These are: purpose, identity, values and beliefs, capabilities, behaviours and environment. These levels represent a natural relationship of social systems, with each level being more abstract then the one below, whilst also having a greater degree of impact on the overall system. The following table elaborates on the logical levels and their corresponding meanings, and uses the example of a shoe manufacturer to illustrate each point.

Dilts' model of logical levels		
Level	*Explanation*	*Provides*
Purpose	Changes and learning relating to the larger system of which the culture or individual is part.	The reason for existing. Defines the organisation's service to the wider community and provides a direction for leadership. e.g. to make feet happy
Identity	Who are we? What is the organisation's role?	A framework for the brand. A feel for the culture. A reason for the symbol or logo. e.g. quality shoe manufacturing
Values and beliefs	What do we believe is most important and why?	Defines the organisation's core beliefs and values, and provides motivation. e.g. profit, innovation, people
Capability	How to make things happen — the competencies, strategies and skills required to deliver what is most important.	Awareness of the resources required to achieve success. Provides guidance for direction. e.g. planning, marketing
Behaviour	What to do — how I am expected to act.	Defines actions and reactions, and is the structure for all job descriptions. Provides the ethical framework for how the values will be expressed. e.g. working from a plan
Environment	External context: competition, market, economy, geographical location.	Where and when I behave, and the typical external environment in which this takes place. Defines the extent and scope of constraints and opportunities. e.g. geographical location

The various levels do not stand alone, nor are they hierarchical as each impacts on the others — they are in fact interdependent. Often, a genuine sense of purpose can only emerge once there is clear understanding of the other levels. However, the items towards the top of the table, such as identity and values, have a far wider and deeper impact on the organisation than the individual facets of the environment. As we move towards the top of the table, each level progressively impacts on more of the overall structure.

If we examine each level in turn, we can see that the organisation can only have a sense of identity once it knows what it stands for, what business it is in, has been named, branded if necessary, and has created a logo and a company story. An interesting point to note, and one that often intrigues our clients, is that profit, shareholder return and growth, do not feature at the level of purpose. To suggest that the sole purpose of being in business is to make a profit would be like saying the sole purpose of being alive is to breathe. Profit-making is a priority and/or a capability, not a purpose.

The next level — values and beliefs — concerns the foundation values of the company. In order to live those values, areas of capability need to be identified. The behaviours necessary to achieve these capabilities are then identified, and further defined in terms of when and where they are to be used.

It is through using this model that an organisation creates alignment between its purpose, its identity, its values, its skills and capabilities, its desired behaviours (as represented through job descriptions) and its relationship to territory, geographical placement, decor, image and even its recycling policies.

The beauty of this approach is that it works equally as well with an individual. The individual simply begins by considering what role they play in the organisation (identity) and begins to map out the requirements of that role using the model. We have used the logical levels model to support leadership development within our clients' organisations.

- The level of purpose involves the *for whom* aspect of the business and its leaders.

- The level of identity involves the *who* of leadership and is related to a mission.

- The level of values and beliefs concerns the *why* of leadership.

- The level of capabilities involves the *how* of leadership.

- The level of behaviour involves the *what* of leadership.

- The level of environment involves the *where* and *when* of leadership.

Once identity has been established, the values in particular have a significant impact on the components selected to complete the remaining structure of the model.

We can see in the following diagram the degree of influence and impact a single value has on the overall structure of the business. The shaded area represents the portion of the overall structure that is influenced by a change in just one belief or value. This shows graphically how important it is to select the most appropriate and aligned values to fit individual or organisational requirements. If one value changes, the following three levels will need to be reviewed. Many organisations underestimate the impact of their choice of values and wonder later why they are having difficulty implementing and aligning values into the business. The figure below shows why the selection and adoption of a values set should not be taken lightly. Values have tremendous benefits

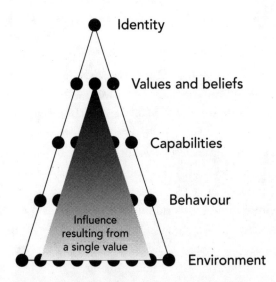

**The amount of influence of a single value
on an organisation's culture**

Identity

Values and beliefs

Capabilities

Behaviour

Influence resulting from a single value

Environment

Adapted with permission from the work of Robert Dilts

to offer the organisation when the organisation's capabilities, behaviour and environment are aligned with them.

Values alignment creates an organisation's culture

Values-based organisations deliver their values through their culture, via their systems and people. The company culture is such that people are aware of their environment and deliberate about their choices. They are not immersed in the culture to the extent that they lose their own identity.

Values provide the only basis for full comprehension of any culture, because to make any sense of a culture we need to understand its values. In fact, all cultures can be defined as a 'living' set of values at work supported and given meaning by an underlying cluster of beliefs.

These values and beliefs are expressed through ritual, customs, laws, ceremony and systems. If values are taken out of the equation when defining a culture, what is left is a confusing, meaningless interaction of relationships without purpose, exchange or outcomes.

Paul Ray and Sherry Anderson, authors of *The Cultural Creatives: How 50 million people are changing the world,* have written a phenomenal book on the scope, power, depth and breadth of new values sets emerging in the USA. They credit values as the most effective way to truly understand a culture and human behaviour. They write, 'You have to go far beyond opinions and attitudes, because these shift as quickly as a summer wind. You have to dive down into the values and world-views that shape people's lives — the deep structure that shifts gradually over decades or generations. Once you catch sight of these deep changes and track them, you can discover a lot about what matters most to people and how they will act. Values are the best single predictor of real behaviour.'

Every company culture evolves out of a set of values at work. These values might not necessarily be the ones the organisation has deliberately chosen; they might in fact be a mixture of the values of previous cultures and the personal values that individuals within the organisation bring to work. If this is the case, then the values that dominate the organisation may not be the ones that management wishes to dominate and guide the company's culture and way of doing business.

Our consulting experience bears this out, regardless of the industry, size and values emphasis of the company. If an organisation does not provide a values framework around which people can rally and aspire to and create a sense of meaning, then people invent their own meaning and use their personal values for making decisions.

An organisation's culture can mean the difference between unparalleled success and uncontrollable failure. So how do we build a strong culture? We start with a strong and appropriate set of values and design systems for people to implement these values. Creating a strong and explicit values set on which the culture will rest is critical to ongoing success. In their book *Built to Last*, Collins and Porras showed that of the companies they researched, the ones that consistently focused on building strong corporate cultures over a period of several decades financially outperformed companies that did not by a factor of 6 and outperformed the general stock market by a factor of 15.

All too often the management and design of organisations' cultures are deemed the sole interest and responsibility of the human resource department; however, it is obvious that culture is the collective responsibility of all involved, particularly the leader. More than anyone else, an organisation's leader influences the flavour and nature of the organisation's culture. Of course, there are external factors such as the economy, politics and the market; however, even these are filtered through the leader's decisions to determine how they will and will not influence the organisation's culture.

Richard Barrett, former values coordinator for the World Bank, makes this observation in *Liberating the Corporate Soul*: 'The fundamental challenge facing business leaders is to create a corporate culture that supports and encourages all employees to tap into their deepest levels of productivity and creativity by finding personal fulfilment through their work. When people find meaning in their work they naturally tap into their deepest levels of creativity and highest levels of productivity.' Once this is achieved, the resulting culture leads the business to success.

Note that it is the culture that leads, not the CEO. In all sustainable, successful organisations it is the values at work in the culture that are the organisation's real leader. Therefore, if the CEO should leave, the organisation still moves ahead by continuing to work with its own values. In *Corporate Culture and Performance*, Kotter and Heskett show that companies with strong adaptive cultures based on shared values outperformed other companies by a significant margin. Measured over an 11-year period, they grew four times faster than companies with no emphasis on these facets of the business.

Values are the invisible threads of an organisation's culture as they connect people, performance and profit. The key to creating such a culture is to link the various logical levels of the organisation to and through the values. You may wish to use the following table to map out the various levels of your organisation and understand their relationship to your values, once you have completed reading the remaining chapters in this part of the book.

Your organisation's logical levels

Purpose	
Identity	
Values and beliefs	
Capabilities	
Behaviour	
Environment	

CHAPTER 8

How to develop the organisation's values

A company's values are the DNA
of its culture.

—

The way some organisations go about creating their values set is often the cause of half the problems they have when implementing them at a later stage. A popular approach to values creation can look something like this:

- The senior management team holds a retreat, where they talk about which values the company wishes to adopt.

- An initial list of the values and their meanings is drawn up.

- After ongoing discussion and a few draft attempts, the values list is signed off by the CEO and senior management team.

- A launch plan, including posters, cards and screensavers, is devised.

- The values are launched using roadshows and seminars.

While this approach looks fairly comprehensive, values created and introduced in this way invariably fail to take root in the business, due to the following steps being overlooked:

- The people creating the values have no common understanding about what values are and what influence they have.

- There is no process for aligning the people and systems in the organisation to the values.

- Values are not used in decision-making.

- The values are not placed in a hierarchy.

- There is no planning for values auditing processes.

- People are not provided with the opportunity to determine their own personal values.

Popular misconceptions

The more people involved in creating the values, the greater the buy-in.
From our experience, it's not about how many people are involved, but rather who is involved. Only employees who play a part in determining the strategy of the organisation can meaningfully contribute to the values creation process. This doesn't necessarily limit participants to the management team — there may be other employees in your organisation who have a strategic role in a defined area. Involving non-strategic employees in values creation is time-consuming, distracting and expensive and has minimal effect on the values being lived in the organisation. However, involving a cross-section of employees is useful for making sure the values are expressed in everyday language.

It takes a lot of time to get the values right.
It often does, but it needn't take a lot of time to get the right values. We often hear horror stories of organisations spending days, weeks or even months on the wording of their values, when we find it usually takes about 6–8 hours to develop an appropriate values set. Spending time aligning the values is far more important than refining the words. Collins, in his paper 'Aligning Action and Values', states that the typical allocation of time taken in values creation and alignment is:

0–5%	90–100%	0–5%
Identifying core values	Drafting and redrafting the statement	Creating alignment

His view of the desired allocation is consistent with our experiences of successfully aligning values at work.

10–20%	0–5%	80–90%
Identifying core values	Drafting and redrafting the statement	Creating alignment

How to develop your organisation's values

The next step in the development of an organisation's values is to brief the senior management team on the nature of values, their definition, benefits, and impact on organisations and culture. We outlined why this is so important in chapter 4. You might consider asking each manager to read this book in preparation for the briefing, so that they may better prepare their thoughts, comments, questions and criticisms. The meeting should specifically seek feedback from this team about the concept of your organisation becoming a values-based organisation.

If it is agreed to go ahead, the next step is to organise a time and place for these managers, or their nominated and interested representatives, to attend a values creation session. Many teams opt to go offsite for two or three days to achieve the best results for the session. This is fine if the team believe they need to be free from interruptions. However, it is not absolutely necessary. We have repeatedly achieved excellent results working with groups on site in a half-day session. Burger King New Zealand's core values — pride passion and performance — were identified in a half-day on-site meeting and have proven to be perfect for their culture and successful for the business in an operational, strategic and human-resource sense. The key to Burger King's values success is they placed more emphasis on the alignment of the values with the values of their people than on the creation of the values.

The key steps of a values creation session are as follows:

Phase 1

1. The group should nominate an experienced facilitator to guide the session. The facilitator needn't be experienced in values — just at facilitating group discussions and tracking feedback. Some notes on guiding sessions are included at the end of this chapter. If there is no one available inside the organisation you may like to consider hiring an external facilitator for the first day.

2. The facilitator should ask the group (or groups if there are over eight people present) to consider and answer the following question: 'What has this organisation always stood for and consistently prioritised, no matter what circumstances it has faced?'

3. The group or groups should capture their responses to this question as keywords; these, along with any explanatory meanings should be written on a flip chart. Allow the groups as much time as they wish to complete their answers.

4. Each group should share their results in an informal presentation to the group as a whole. It's vital that this happens in a non-judgemental environment and that the keywords and their meanings are understood by everyone.

5. The facilitator should next ask the group as a whole to review the results of the presentations. In particular the participants should look for overlaps between values. For example, one group may have come up with a value of 'service', meaning, 'to provide our customers with timely and optimum results'. A second group might have identified a value of 'customer service' meaning, 'to meet or exceed customer expectations'. The group should note the overlap, similarity or relationship between the two values (and any other similar values) and write the most popular wording and expression of the value on a separate sheet of paper. This needn't be the finished definition of the value, or even be grammatically accurate at this stage. All that is required is that the values and their general meaning have been captured and are available for further exploration at a later stage.

6. The facilitator should then guide the group through the same process, only this time addressing a new question: 'What will we choose to, or need to, prioritise from now on as an organisation in order to achieve our purpose?' Repeat the question three more times, substituting vision, mission and strategies for purpose.

7. The facilitator should next guide the group through a comparison of the lists, identifying any overlaps. Any overlapping values can be combined or their meanings adjusted to incorporate both ideas, and capture more precisely the group's thinking and feelings about what is most important.

8. Once overlaps have been combined or deleted, the final list of values should be studied for its appropriateness and expression. If possible, try to reduce your list of final values to five values or less. Organisations with more than five values are rarely able to have them all recalled by all their employees.

Phase 2

Discuss the underlying beliefs around the selected values. This process is outlined in chapter 9.

Phase 3

If you have more than three values, arrange the values list into an order of priority. This is discussed in chapter 10.

Phase 4

When the list has been agreed and prioritised, the group should consider the consequences of both running the business and basing all decisions on these values. Read chapter 11 on values and decision-making prior to commencing this stage. To thoroughly test these values, review any particularly challenging times or incidents that the organisation has faced and consider how these values might have stood up in such situations. Similarly the group should consider a series of successful and unsuccessful decisions that have been made in the past and evaluate whether these decisions honoured or dishonoured these values. Typically, successful decisions will have honoured the values selected even though the values had not then been articulated. Finally, the values should be tested for their overall ability — given the foreseeable future — to move the organisation towards achieving its vision. If the values appear suitable for all these considerations the group can celebrate the creation of a values set.

Phase 5

Getting feedback from all employees is optional, and depends on the size and geographical dispersion of the organisation. If any comments arise from feedback that have not been already discussed by the values project team, then members of that team should reconvene to evaluate the impact of these comments using the process outlined above.

Once the values have been agreed upon, the process for launching and aligning the values within the business can be planned and executed.

Phase 6

The internal marketing of values often becomes the focal point for organisations attempting to launch their values. It's as if they think that printing and distributing posters of the organisation's values will instantly see them embraced by staff. Other ideas we've seen include distributing mouse pads, screensavers, T-shirts, caps, coffee mugs and bumper stickers to ensure that the values aren't forgotten. These items certainly assist in the introduction of the values into company culture, but it would be naïve to think that's all that's required.

Our experience suggests that in many respects, internal marketing is often over-emphasised in building a values-based organisation. However, the desire to make values — which by definition are intangible — tangible and visible is quite understandable. On its own, though, such marketing is a pointless exercise. We have seen organisations spend small fortunes on such launches and then watched as the embodiment of the values fell through because some of the all-important steps discussed in this book were not included in the process. Chief among these is the failure to support employees to clarify their own personal values and learn how best to align these values with those of the organisation.

In summary, marketing exercises will aid the success of a values launch if and only if they are recognised as part of the process and not the process in its entirety.

Phase 7

Aligning the personal values of employees with the organisation is the most commonly neglected step, but it is critical to the success of a values programme. This is discussed in chapter 13.

Tips for clarifying your organisation's values

- Don't pretend to be something you're not. If you are all about competing and surviving then don't be afraid to say so in your values. Don't disguise who you really are under a list of politically correct values you don't agree with.

- Be S.M.A.R.T. with your values. Smart stands for **S**hort, **M**eaningful, **A**rticulate, **R**elevant, and **T**ransactional.

   S No matter what values you end up with, try to ensure you do not have more than five at the end of the process. People struggle to remember more than this, and trying to align the organisation to more than five values can be unwieldy and awkward.

   M Make sure the values are meaningful to people, so that employees will be motivated to behave in alignment with the values. Profit, for example, may not always inspire people within the business, especially if they receive no share of any increase in the profits they are working to achieve.

   A When you finalise a value ensure it is memorable and easily understood by staff. For example, Burger King has defined its value of passion as 'Live it'. In other words, they encourage their staff, many of whom are teenagers, to live the energy and enthusiasm of the brand within their role. Another organisation we worked with defined profit as 'It gives us our grunt'. Our organisation, Values@work, defines profit as '*Pro*fessional *Fit*ness'. These definitions enable people working within the business to buy in to the company values.

   R The values should be relevant to the business. There is no use having a value of 'collaboration' if the functions of the business are very much stand-alone and independence is one of the organisation's strengths. Similarly, 'creativity' is not relevant if the organisation is focused on simply maintaining a steady line of production within tight timeframes.

T Make sure people are able to transfer the meaning of each value into specific behaviours within their role. For example, the organisation may attach the meaning 'earnings exceed costs by 10 per cent' to the value of profit, and employees will need to use specific behaviours to achieve this.

Evaluating your values

If some people express doubt about whether a suggested value is really what the organisation wants to stand for, a useful exercise to carry out is the neurolinguistic programming exercise known as Cartesian coordinates.

The group asks the following four questions, to enable them to look at the potential results from different viewpoints.

1. What do we get if we adopt and align with this value?

2. What do we get if we don't adopt and align with this value?

3. What don't we get if we adopt and align with this value?

4. What don't we get if we don't adopt and align with this value?

We have on numerous occasions seen this process uncover important issues that probably would otherwise not have been realised or discussed.

Finally it is inevitable that there will be much thinking, rationalising, considering, debating and even arguing as the group work their way through the values creation process. A key point to keep in mind is to pay attention to your own feelings. Ask yourself in relation to the values, 'What feels right?' Pay attention to when the group seems to click or becomes positively energised around a value.

Tips on guiding a values-creation session

In a guided session to create company values, a group of people are active participants in a process that aims to achieve agreed predetermined outcomes. They are overseen by a 'guide' or facilitator, who focuses the group more on the content to be covered than the immediate desires of the participants.

This is not intended as a comprehensive guide to facilitating, but should be sufficient to give an overview of the process.

Prior to the session

1. Have all participants read this book.

2. Find a venue for the session that you believe is conducive to the work being undertaken.

3. Make sure you have everything you need for the session.

4. Focus on where your attention is and how you are feeling prior to opening the session, to ensure you are focusing on the task at hand.

Opening the session

1. Go round the group giving each person the opportunity to say a few words about where their attention is at the moment and what they can do to focus on the session. For example, a participant might say, 'I was rushed for a parking space and I'm still thinking about what I need to have brought, I just need a moment or two to relax.'

2. Clarify the purpose of the session. Give each participant the chance to voice any alternative views or thoughts they have on the purpose of the session.

3. Have the group explore how individual viewpoints influence the progress of discussions and decision-making. If the group already works effectively as a team you may skip this and the next two steps.

4. Determine how individuals feel about expressing what they really want to say rather than voicing what they feel is the 'party line'.

5. Explore with the group the value of having agreed guidelines for running the session and how they will apply them.

6. Lead a group discussion about everyone's understanding of values and their importance to the business. This should be based on the reading that was done by all participants prior to the meeting.

During the session

1. Keep the participants focused on making a constructive contribution. Asking a question like 'How does this contribute to achieving our purpose?' helps keep people focused on what's being created.

2. Create a 'car park' for questions or points raised that are related to values creation/application but not relevant to the immediate work being undertaken. The 'car park' can be emptied at the end of the day.

3. Give everyone the opportunity to contribute to the discussion. This can be done by:
   — creating small discussion groups that report their findings to the whole group (this is an option even with a group of four or five people).
   — giving people time on their own to write their thoughts down and then go round each person in the group for their feedback. Make sure each person finishes what they have to say before discussions take place.
   — having people put information on whiteboards and present it to the group.
   — asking dominant contributors to allow two other people to respond before they contribute their view.

4. Have any questions you are going to ask the group to answer prepared in a visual format (e.g. flip chart). When appropriate, display the question for participants to keep in sight while working.

5. At every stage where an agreement is reached, document what's been agreed in a way that is visible for all to see.

6. Recap where the group is up to at regular intervals so everyone is in step.

7. Have regular hourly breaks to give people an opportunity to re-energise.

Closing the session

1. Review all the information agreed upon with the group.

2. Check where you are up to in the values creation process. If the creation process is unfinished, set a mutually convenient time for the next session.

3. Empty the 'car park'. Review any unfinished topics or unanswered questions and agree any actions required to be taken to address them.

4. Agree who gets a copy of what.

5. Agree the next steps.

6. Give everyone the uninterrupted opportunity to express how they feel about the session and acknowledge what they have achieved.

7. Celebrate.

CHAPTER 9

Aligning beliefs around your values

When aligned around shared values and united in a common mission, ordinary people accomplish extraordinary things.

Ken Blanchard and Michael O'Connor, *Managing by Values*

—

Although this book is focused on the role and benefits of values in organisations, the real power of values resides in the beliefs that support and underlie them. The more a value is believed to be important by the people in an organisation, the more motivated they will be to behave in a manner that is congruent with that value. Behaviour emanates from values.

One of the reasons so many values initiatives fail to survive much longer than the values launch is that people within the organisation are not provided with an opportunity to align their beliefs with the values. Facilitating the alignment of beliefs to the company values enables the values to be successfully assimilated into people's work lives.

What management driving cultural change often don't understand is a value is only a genuine value of the organisation when it is voluntarily chosen and acted upon by the people. The typical approach organisations take towards values and beliefs is to nominate the value and assume that people will naturally adopt the most appropriate supporting beliefs about that value. In reality, however, the beliefs of the company are often anything but supporting. The following diagram indicates some possible unaligned beliefs around the company value of integrity. You can see these are hardly the attitudes management had in mind when they selected integrity as one of the company's values.

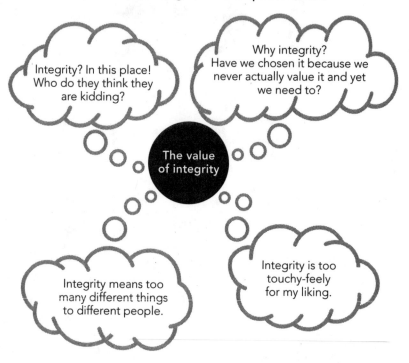

A value with unaligned and unspoken beliefs

How to align beliefs to your organisation's values

To create an aligned belief around a value is a complex (although not complicated) process best initiated in a workshop format. The process, known as 'believing the value', is one of the most critical aspects for ensuring the values are understood, accepted and chosen by the people working for the company. The process ensures that instead of many unspoken and shared beliefs about the value, there is one predominant belief about the value that is agreed upon and communicated by all.

The process has a way of really bringing the value to life, as it charges the value with the energy of commitment and shared belief. This creates greater alignment and personal motivation to live the value. It also provides greater understanding of what the organisation stands for in each individual's mind. By comparison, the end result looks like the process outlined in the following figure. When beliefs are aligned around a value, everyone in the company shares the same enthusiasm and commitment to living the value, as shown in the diagram below.

A value with aligned beliefs

To ensure the value is embodied by everyone, it's necessary to create an aligned belief structure to support the value.

The belief alignment process

The group working on creating company values also needs to ensure their beliefs around those values are aligned, using the following process.

1. The facilitator should select a value and ask the group to complete the following sentence: 'We value integrity [or whatever the value is] because . . .'

   For example, 'We value profit because it keeps us going, or we value profit because we deserve to succeed.' The facilitator should write down all of the participants' answers on a whiteboard or flip chart.

2. When the group has exhausted all its ideas, the facilitator should read the list back to them and ask for their reactions to the statements one by one. The facilitator should explain to the group that it is the energy of the statement that gives the value its grunt, and that this is what the group should consider, rather than logical or rational analysis. Any statement that meets with *any* dissatisfaction from *any* group member should be eliminated from the list.

3. This process should continue until a unanimous decision has been reached on the most meaningful and energising statement of all those initially presented. The belief statement is then written down beneath the value and its meaning. If all the beliefs are rejected, start the process again, or reword a belief until it is acceptable to everyone.

4. Repeat the process for the next value until all five values are completed.

Our organisation, values@work, operates with the following five values: purpose, relating, profit, work smart and allegria. The values, their meanings and motivating beliefs are set out below.

Value	Meaning	Belief
Purpose	Making life meaningful	Purpose provides a reason for being
Relating	Sharing enthusiasm	Provides enriched experiences
Profit	Professional fitness	Provides ability to be here now and in the future
Work smart	Optimum input, optimum output	Provides experience and results easily and effortlessly
Allegria	Making it simple and fun	Provides enjoyment and fulfilment

Every time we have worked through this process with a group, people have commented on how powerful the experience was. To feel a group of people align on a single and unanimously agreed belief about a value is unifying and empowering. It also has an added benefit of being a wonderful team-building experience.

Of course, people believing in the values is only half of the journey. The next step is to place them in a hierarchy.

CHAPTER 10

Placing values
in a hierarchy

The most important thing is to know
what is the most important thing.

—

Values are very rarely equal. Depending on the context and the organisation's overall purpose, one value will usually be considered more important than the others, even if only by a marginal degree.

Milton Rokeach, in *The Nature of Human Values*, makes an amazing and potentially alarming comment about the number of variations that can result from having values without hierarchy: 'A mere dozen and a half terminal values for instance can be arranged in order of importance in 18 factorial ways, which comes to over 640 trillion different ways.' Failure to prioritise your values can and often does lead to organised chaos, because each individual can potentially interpret the relative importance of an organisation's values for themselves in their own unique order. Remember, however, your organisation should ideally choose no more than five values.

An organisation we worked with some years ago had the following values: profit, growth, safety, integrity and quality customer service. We were invited to assist them in overcoming continual internal conflict that resulted from people making decisions based on a value that conflicted or even contradicted one of the other values. Our first task was to ask the senior management team what order of priority each of them would place the values. In no time at all, the four managers had come up with four different orders of priority for the values, as follows:

Sales Manager	Finance Manager	HR Manager	Operations Manager
Profit	Growth	Safety	Growth
Growth	Profit	Integrity	Safety
Safety	Quality	Quality	Profit
Integrity	Integrity	Profit	Quality
Quality	Safety	Growth	Integrity

Straightaway, the reasons for the internal conflict became obvious. The sales manager and her team were making all their decisions focusing primarily on making a profit, to ensure growth. While safety, integrity and quality were recognised as important, they were secondary to profit in her eyes.

Alternatively, the HR manager and his team were making decisions based primarily on safety and integrity, to the extent that ensuring safety may in fact reduce the overall profit of the organisation.

The two values sets look very similar and yet as a day-to-day experience, they were producing significant internal conflict between departments. It wasn't that one manager's values set was better than another — it was a case of clarifying what was most important to the business.

To resolve the conflict, the organisation needed to prioritise the values in order to clearly express its preferred way of operating. Failure to specifically identify the desired priority meant that the values hierarchy was being chosen indiscriminately through the day-to-day choices of its managers.

The management team recognised this and we set about working with them to identify a single order of priority that met everyone's needs. This step often requires considerable effort from the group members, who must be willing to consider viewpoints other than their own. The facilitator has an important role to play in this, by reminding the group (often regularly) that the values represent the whole organisation's overall priorities and preferences, not just the desires the department or function of the individual represented in the session.

Once everyone agrees on the order the values should be placed in, the overall values process will begin to flourish as potential values conflict will be largely avoided in the future. In the case of the management team discussed here, the result of the group prioritising their values meant that within a 90-day period, all the original conflicts had been resolved and new conflicts arose only occasionally.

Robert Fritz offers a number of guiding principles for achieving forward momentum in organisational structure. One of his principles is known as the senior organising principle. Fritz writes, 'When a senior organising principle is absent, the organisation will oscillate. When a senior organising principle is dominant, the organisation will advance.' This is exactly what our client experienced, because without assigning priority to the organisation's values, chaos had ensued. Once the values had been prioritised, the organisation could move forward.

How to prioritise your organisation's values

Prioritising your organisation's values is particularly important if you have more than three values. If your organisation has only three values see the option outlined on page 114. The same group creating the organisation's values should continue with the prioritisation exercise below.

For organisations with more than three values

1. Write the values (and their meanings) on separate pieces of paper and place Blu-Tack or some other adhesive on the back of each piece.

2. Ask the question, 'Which of these values is the most important for everyone to be focused on?' (i.e. our vision, mission or what we stand for). When you have agreed majority consensus, select the value that is most popular for the time being and place this value on the wall or flip chart.

3. Repeat the question with the remaining values for the second most important value, then the third and so on until all values have been ranked.

4. When you have placed the values in this initial rough order of priority, use the following question to determine if any of the values need to change position: 'If we were fully experiencing value A, could we live without everyone being focused on value B?' This does not mean you would want to do without value B — you are just trying to confirm which is more important.

   If the answer is the value currently ranked first, then move on and compare the second value with the third (using the same question). If the answer again is 'the higher value', then repeat the process for the third and fourth value.

   If on the other hand, the answer to the question comparing value one with value two is value two, swap value one with value two and repeat the question.

   If the order of the values changes, you will need to re-evaluate the newly positioned value with those above it.

   Do not be surprised if this leads to a significant shift in the order of the values. Similarly, do not be surprised if it does not!

5. If for any reason the group becomes stuck in this evaluation process then ask the question, 'Which of these two values is going to have the most influence on focusing our attention on our objective?' (i.e. the company's vision, mission or purpose). Whichever value is nominated as the most influential becomes the higher value.

6. When the group believes it has finalised the hierarchy, run through the process again to ensure there is total agreement at each level. Consider re-ordering the values again to take into account different perspectives and viewpoints; evaluate the results of this as a group.

7. When the values hierarchy is complete it is then time to consider how the values will be assimilated into the business through decision-making, aligning behaviours, internal marketing coaching and recruitment, all of which are covered in subsequent chapters.

For organisations with three values

When an organisation has only three values, they may find it difficult to prioritise them, although it is not impossible.

When this is the case, the organisation may choose to model the overlap relationship between the three values. This model recognises that all three values are of almost equal importance, and shows how they contribute to the overall objective. This was what happened when Burger King identified its values. It was decided that the three values contributed equally to the organisation's overall purpose. No one value was seen as dominating the values process. When an organisation's values are grouped in this manner, it is known as a values constellation, which is represented graphically in the figure below. A good analogy is a constellation of stars, where no one star within the constellation is deemed to be significantly more important than any other. All the individual stars contribute to the overall shape of the constellation. Similarly, in a values constellation, all of the individual values contribute to achieving the company's vision.

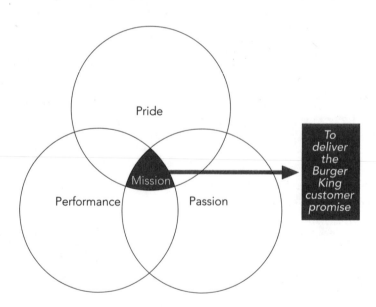

CHAPTER 11

Values-based decision-making

Situations involving fully conscious choice reveal that,
in the last resort, every choice of one and not another
possible way of acting is psychologically grounded
in evaluation — even if the agent is not aware of
such dependence.

Z. Najder, *Values and Evaluation*

For any organisation to operate in alignment with its values, people
need to make decisions based on those values. The company's values
provide a decision-making guideline for all the departments that make
up the company structure. However if the company's values are not
clearly articulated and understood, then people are more likely to base
their decisions on their own values rather than those of the organisation.
The more employees understand the organisation's values, the more
aligned their decision-making will be.

There are immense benefits to be gained from understanding that
decision-making is a values-based process. Our experience has shown
that high-performance companies have a clear set of values that
underpin decision-making at all levels.

People, values and systems

From a values perspective, an organisation comprises three components:
people, values and systems.

People are, of course, the driving force within the business, as they choose the organisation's values either deliberately or unconsciously, and also develop, implement and monitor the systems.

Values, as we have seen, are priorities and preferences. They are our reason for being in business. They represent our underlying reasoning and our desired outcome from the business. They also define the way we want to do business.

Systems are ways of doing and achieving things. It is the systems that enable us to achieve our values as specific outcomes. Systems and values are complementary parts of the organisation's culture. If the system is not delivering our preferred outcome, then intervening decisions need to be taken to realign the systems.

The running, direction and control of a business is dependent on a variety of systems, for example a system to generate sales, production systems, and systems for marketing, research and development and finance. These systems are run by people, who interact with them through the decisions they make on a daily basis.

Decision-making is the most fundamental connection between values and systems. Values and systems interact through decisions. Values are central to understanding and interacting with any system, because they provide the relevant filters through which the system and its progress or outcomes are evaluated.

A system can be said to be performing unsatisfactorily when it is not delivering the desired outcomes in terms of factors such as efficiency, productivity and quality. Likewise, a system is deemed to be performing or functioning when it is achieving these criteria. The things we are evaluating the system for, such as efficiency, profit, creativity, information, quality and the like, are in fact values.

The diagram on the next page represents this process and the paths of interaction.

As systems are designed to create outcomes, decisions are constantly required to ensure the system is producing the right results, at the right time, in the right manner. Feedback from systems can help us to realign our systems to our values. If we value 'productivity' and we have feedback from the system that informs us 'productivity' is not being achieved, then we are able to make a decision about what could be done to address the situation.

Systems, values and decision-making

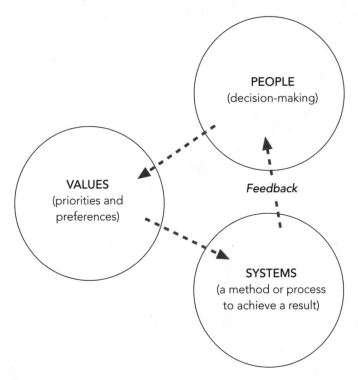

Decisions are based more on values than rational analysis

It is tempting to view all decision-making as predominantly rational and logical analysis of data. However, research by Peters and Waterman indicates that decisions are based more on priority values than on rational analysis. It seems that decision-making is based on factual data overlaid by an emotional context. The data is what indicates a decision needs to be made and it can influence the way we implement the decision. The values are the emotional filters through which we make the decision.

In *The Winning Streak Mark 2*, Goldsmith and Clutterbuck quote research into how the brain functions: 'The neocortex, the seat of rational analysis, provides us with the ability to establish and respond to rules.' They go on to explain that this allows us to reason, ponder and analyse. 'On its own, however, it is useless. People who are unfortunate enough to lose access to their limbic brain and have to rely on their neocortex prove unable to make even simple decisions. It seems that we need an overlay of emotional context to make rational judgements.'

This emotional context is how we determine the relative importance of the material about which we are making the decisions. In other words, if we didn't value profit or productivity to begin with, we would not be concerned about financial losses.

In fact, many people in organisations, particularly at an operational level, are often baffled as to why the company has asked them to cut back on the use of some internal resource or to delay the purchase of new equipment. These staff, who may not relate the value of profit to these type of decisions, do not see the logic of the organisation's reasoning. This is because the staff members are viewing the decision through their own values filters, for example, competency (i.e. 'I could do my job more effectively if you would just buy me a new laptop computer') or competition (i.e. 'Why should I cut back on the use of the quality watermarked paper for my proposals to customers when our opposition use high-quality paper?').

Unless the organisation's high-priority values are known, understood and accepted by all people in the organisation, decision-making will predominantly be based on the values chosen by the individual, which may have an overall fragmenting impact on the business. Each individual's decision may, in fact, inadvertently sabotage the organisation's overall priorities.

For example, imagine the situation where a senior manager is concerned about the high cost of using quality paper for client proposal documents. The manager feels this does not productively and profitably contribute to the securing of client contacts. However, the sales representative might be concerned about the perceived lowering of quality in the eyes of the customer if lower-grade paper is used. They may feel it places the company at a disadvantage to the competition.

If the organisation operates without a predetermined values hierarchy, then the manager's decision to use inferior paper will likely result in resentment as the salesperson places a higher value on quality and service than on profitability. The manager, on the other hand, sees profitability as the overriding value at stake.

However, when the organisation's values are known to all people, then everyone is able to make decisions in alignment with the organisation's best interests. Company values need to be included in the decision-making process, as indicated in the diagram below.

Values-based decision model for an organisation

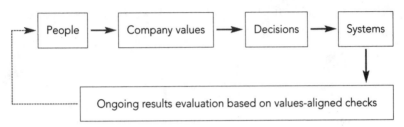

In summary, if the organisation does not clarify and communicate its values, then by default it is assumed they are understood. In reality they remain tacit in nature. This results in people basing their decisions on their own selection of values rather than those that are in the organisation's strategic interests. This is illustrated in the diagram below.

The impact of the absence of explicit organisational values on decision-making

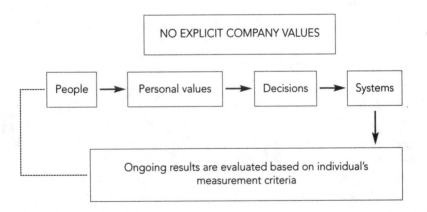

In our experience, managers and employees make more decisions aligned with the company's best interest when they have a clear understanding of the company values. In their book *Hidden Value*, O'Reilly and Pfeffer report on the extraordinary success experienced by the Southwestern airlines, commenting: 'Their success comes not from some secret, but from the exquisite attention they (and the other firms we describe) pay to aligning their values with systems, structure and strategy.'

How to base all decisions on your organisation's values

To successfully implement a values-based decision-making process in an organisation, people must constantly refer to the organisation's explicit set of values when deciding what action to take, strategy to adopt or investment to approve.

We have found the following steps effective in creating a situation where all decisions are based on the organisation's values.

1. Firstly, the organisation must have established and explicitly defined its values.

2. Once the values have been established, short sessions should be run for all managers and employees to discuss the process of basing decisions on the organisation's values. Typical situations that arise in each of the various departments should be discussed and the values to identify solutions applied. For example, if the organisation's values were profit, quality, innovation and performance, the group should consider and review how, for any decisions they are required to make, they might ensure these decisions support the company values. The suggestions should then be evaluated by the group in terms of their degree of alignment to the values to determine the idea's appropriateness. In this manner, ideal decision criteria can be established while the staff get the opportunity to practise their decision-making skills in a no-risk environment.

3. At weekly team meetings, managers should direct their staff's attention to the values posted on the wall of their meeting room, when discussing solutions to problems. Values-based coaching, which is discussed in chapter 16, may also be helpful in developing competency in decision-making.

4. Introduce employees to the 'I do' concept:

$$Incident \ + \ Decision \ = \ Outcome$$

Incident refers to any given situation where a decision is needed. The decision is the only part of the process individuals have any control over. Choosing how to respond to an incident will determine the outcome. Using values in the decision-making process will ensure the outcome is in line with the organisation's agreed direction.

These sessions build the company culture and empower employees to incorporate the values into their day-to-day decision-making. By also ensuring all people have clarified their own personal values, the organisation can further ensure it has done everything in its power to avoid any values conflicts within the workplace.

Avoiding oscillating decisions

When a senior organisational principle is absent, the organisation will oscillate. When a senior organising principle is dominant, the organisation will advance.

In *The Path of Least Resistance for Managers*, Robert Fritz talks about the theory of oscillating decisions. He suggests that when you take the time to decide what is most important for your organisation, then metaphorically you are moving from a rocking chair (one step forward, one step back) into a car (forward controlled movement towards your destination). The rocking chair is analogous to an organisation that constantly changes its mind about what's important. For example, a company may firstly decide to centralise its business to improve its productivity and profit margins. Two years later, it then decides to decentralise the business to improve customer service and rapid response decision-making. Later, it decides to centralise again to improve quality management's initiatives and productivity.

This regular changing of direction and prioritising fits Fritz's definition of an organisation caught in an oscillating pattern. Other examples of oscillation include employees being asked to take risks, and then later to closely follow directions from senior management, or phases of cost-cutting, then investment. Fritz suggests, 'In these types of oscillating patterns the organisation squanders money, time resources, intellectual capital, morale, reputation and market share, not to mention that it seems to be suffering from manic depression ... [These patterns] exist because of a fundamental structure in which the path of least resistance makes it easy to support first one course of action, strategy, or tactic, but then later its opposite. I call this structural conflict.'

Structural conflicts

Structural conflict is illustrated in the following example. Hunger is caused by a tension between the body's desired amount of food and the actual amount of food available. This tension is resolved by eating until the actual and desired amounts of food are the same.

Fritz has identified that oscillation patterns are produced by two competing tension resolution patterns based on two competing goals. A competing structural tension pattern occurs when we are hungry and eat, yet we are also overweight and wish to diet. In other words, each system conflicts with the other as it tries to achieve its goal. In this example, the first and dominant tension is hunger. To resolve this tension we eat. Once we have eaten, our hunger is diminished and because of what we eat, when we eat and how much we eat, many of us end up gaining weight. Displeasure at being overweight causes us to limit our food intake, thereby causing hunger. The hunger tension thus re-establishes its dominant pattern and as a result we eat.

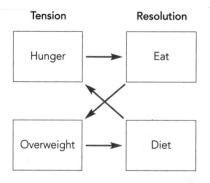

We have come across many examples of oscillating patterns in the course of our work, some of which are illustrated opposite:

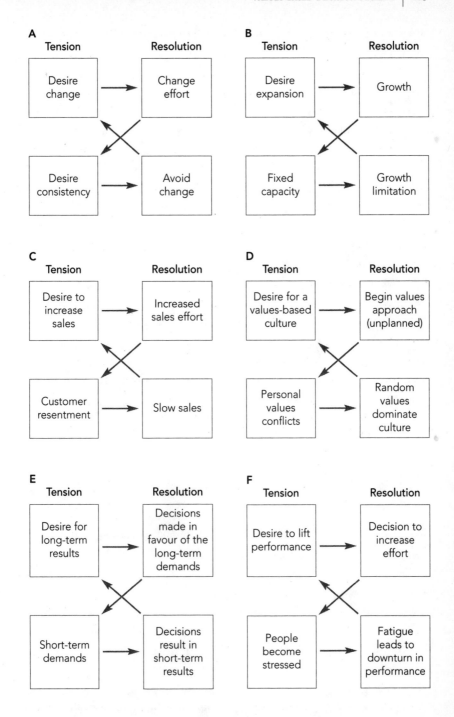

A

Tension | Resolution

Desire change → Change effort

Desire consistency → Avoid change

B

Tension | Resolution

Desire expansion → Growth

Fixed capacity → Growth limitation

C

Tension | Resolution

Desire to increase sales → Increased sales effort

Customer resentment → Slow sales

D

Tension | Resolution

Desire for a values-based culture → Begin values approach (unplanned)

Personal values conflicts → Random values dominate culture

E

Tension | Resolution

Desire for long-term results → Decisions made in favour of the long-term demands

Short-term demands → Decisions result in short-term results

F

Tension | Resolution

Desire to lift performance → Decision to increase effort

People become stressed → Fatigue leads to downturn in performance

How to resolve structural conflicts

Fritz says the way to break out of the oscillation loop within an organisation is to create what he calls a 'hierarchy of importance'. This means we pick one structural goal as being more important than the other. In doing so we make the second one subordinate to the first and then manage the consequences of choosing the first. He says, 'Once we determine which is more important we can redesign the structure by establishing goals that reflect our hierarchy of values.'

For example if we choose to place more importance on satisfying our hunger, then we can begin to manage our behaviour more effectively, by ensuring we do not fall into the patterns of unhealthy eating that lead to weight gain. By relating the goal to our values of, say, health and wellbeing, we can change our behaviour and choose to eat healthier food in appropriate proportions.

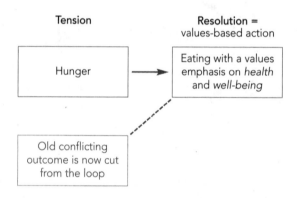

When we alter our behaviour to reflect our values, we begin to make decisions based on our highest priorities. This reduces the impact and influence of subordinate goals to the extent they may even cease to have any impact as long as we maintain our values at the forefront of our decision-making. In this we successfully break the pattern of oscillating and move into the more desirable and productive advancing patterns.

An example of this approach applied to a business situation is outlined on the next page.

The oscillating pattern has been broken by managing the increased sales efforts in alignment with the company's values of customer service and integrity.

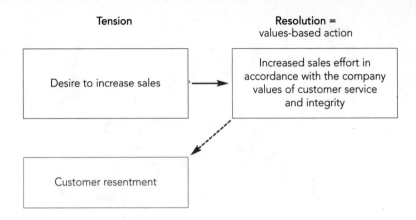

Tension

Resolution =
values-based action

Desire to increase sales

Increased sales effort in
accordance with the company
values of customer service
and integrity

Customer resentment

CHAPTER 12

Linking values and performance

Values are our unconscious motivators —
they determine whether we have the
will to act.

Paul Chippendale, *New Wisdom II*

—

Values can be experienced in different ways — cognitively, emotionally and behaviourally.

Values are experienced cognitively when a person knows or understands why the value is important and they think in alignment with the value. An example of a cognitive value experience is when a person decides that the value of empathy would be important to apply in a given situation to resolve tension in a relationship.

A value can be said to be emotional when we have feelings about the value and the consequences of experiencing it. In this case, the decision to apply the value of empathy is actually experienced as empathy. The person delivering empathy feels empathetic.

A value is behavioural when it leads a person to act according to that value, and yet not necessarily feel the way the value indicates they should, or understand why they're expressing that value. So, a person may act in an empathetic manner, without feeling empathy or understanding why they are acting that way.

These three different ways of experiencing values have important connotations for organisations interested in achieving a high level of performance and high degree of values alignment. People's performance always comprises at least one of these three components. Each component is both an independent and interdependent entity, relying equally on one another for full performance potential to emerge. We refer to these three components as the head, heart and hands of performance.

Head, heart and hands

'Wholeness' is not a commonly held company value, yet if we consider the ramifications of operating an organisation without wholeness, it appears totally irrational. The following model, which we have called 'head, heart and hands', is adapted from work by Paul Chippendale on the research of Paul Tossey and Peter Smith into a 'New Science' organisational behavioural platform, an approach based on a model of organisations viewed as energies of consciousness.

According to this model, performance is dependent on three elements — focus, will and capability, or as we prefer to call them, head, heart and hands. The relationship between these three components is shown in the following diagram.

Head, heart and hands

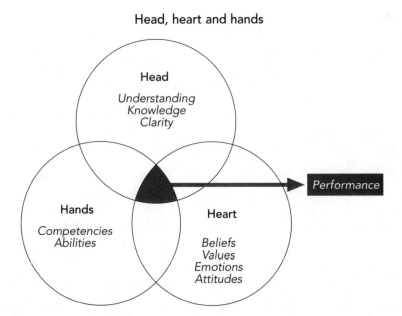

The head represents understanding performance requirements and distinctions, including what, when, how and why things are to be done. Tossey and Smith note individuals and groups may exhibit this by saying:

- I have a good idea of how our company is meeting its competitive challenges.

- Our team's goals for the future have been made clear to me.

- We all know the best way to go about getting our team's work done.

- I am fully aware of how my contribution is valued.

- Our team has full access to information we need to do our job well.

The heart represents the will to act, the beliefs, values, passion, commitment, drive and desire to perform. This could include:

- The work my team and I do is meaningful.

- I feel a strong sense of belonging to this organisation.

- We put in extra effort when we get behind schedule.

- The company and I believe in substantially aligned values.

- I feel the organisation can be trusted to have my best interests at heart.

The hands represent the capability, or skill set, and key performance indicators, for example:

- The team and I have the relevant skills to do our job.

- Resources are made available when required for unexpected priority work and scheduling.

- Management is organised and effective.

- I am fully trained for my role and receive up-skilling and support as and when required.

- Our team is excellent at what we do.

Combinations of the Head, Heart, Hands model

When a person has the hands component (capability) and head (focus) but no heart (will), it usually means they could act but will probably not do so because they have no personal motivation or beliefs that indicate it's worthy to do so.

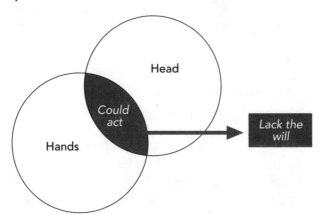

When a person has the head and heart component (focus and will) but no hands (capability), they would act but can't because they do not know how.

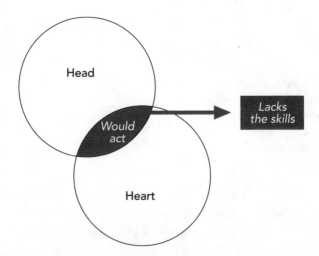

When a person has the hands and heart component (capability and will) but no head (focus), they might act but probably won't because they do not know the requirements process, information or context of the job.

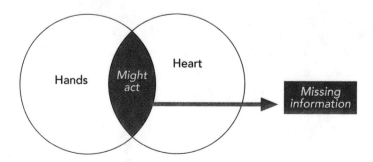

It is only when the head, heart and hands components work together that we act effectively. Values are important to this process because:

1. We attain focus through clarity about our personal and organisational values.

2. We are most motivated to do things which match our personal values and are aligned with the values of our organisation.

3. We prefer to gain skills and abilities around things relating to our personal values.

When we have clear focus, a strong will and capability to act, we are in tune with our values and following the path of least resistance.

The diagram on the next page outlines how each of these components overlap to provide the necessary ingredients for successful performance.

To understand the model, imagine any role or function within your organisation. For example, imagine the role of a sales representative. In order for an individual to be able to deliver high performance in this role, they are required to:

• Understand the role that is required of them (head): including product knowledge, competition, how to follow the company's sales procedures.

• Exhibit emotional maturity (heart): be focused, passionate, behave appropriately, show a positive attitude, be motivated, driven, have a good work ethic, handle knockbacks, be honest and a team player.

- Demonstrate competency (hands): be able to conduct and carry out effectively all the necessary skills required to be a salesperson in your organisation, such as finding new clients, making appointments, conducting presentations, handling objections, closing the sale, typing a proposal or letter, tracking sales progress on the database and so on.

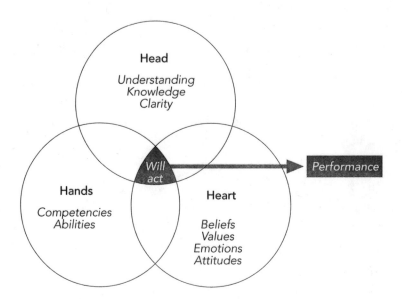

The ability to be and do all these components enables the individual to perform. In the diagram above, this is represented by the inner area labelled 'will act'. This means that the person has all three prerequisite components for sales performance.

Difficulty arises when one of these three components is weak or missing altogether. In the sales representative example, a missing component will result in the following behaviour:

Head and hands without heart
If the individual is lacking 'heart', they could act, because they have the skills and understanding, but they lack motivation or connection with the role, company clients or product; in other words, a critical emotional aspect is missing. Until this situation is resolved, they will not perform to their potential.

Heart and head without hands

If the individual is lacking 'hands', they would act if they could, but they do not know how. They have yet to receive their sales training, or have received it and have difficulty applying it. Again, it is only once this issue is addressed that we can expect high performance.

Hands and heart without head

If the individual is lacking 'head', they would act if they understood what was required of them and could see the reason for doing so. The sales representative might require further understanding of company policy, discount packages, territory guidelines, product information, etc. The individual also needs to understand why they are living the company values. This will be answered when the individual's personal values align with those of the company.

How to link values to performance

1. Run focus sessions with people throughout the organisation to help them link the organisation's values to the head, heart and hands components of their role.

2. Ensure people have clarified their personal values (see chapter 13) and identified any potential conflicts between their values and those of the organisation. Help them to formulate action plans to resolve these conflicts.

CHAPTER 13

Helping people to clarify their own values

Great people want to work at places where they can
actually use their talents, where they are treated
with dignity, trust, and respect, and where they
are engaged by the values and culture of
the organisation.

Charles O'Reilly and Jeffrey Pfeffer, *Hidden Value*

—

In order to align their behaviours with the company's values, employees
first need an understanding of their personal values. Research by Posner
and Schmidt notes that 'clarity about personal values is more important
to our job commitment than clarity about our company values'. Their
research suggests, 'Greater clarity about personal values increases
commitment by 30 per cent.'

The personal values of people working inside your organisation are
important for several reasons. Firstly, they are the filters used by people
to relate to and judge the appropriateness of the organisation's values.
For example, an individual with a high priority on the value of integrity
may express scepticism about the organisation's values being realistic or
the feasibility of them being put into practice. In other words, they
would not want to adopt a value they felt would not be delivered in
practice, because to do so would be hypocritical and lack integrity.
Hence, they express their scepticism.

In order for individuals to align themselves with an organisation's values, they need to be able to identify for themselves how their own personal values can benefit from delivering the company values.

The second reason for the importance of personal values is that personal values are what motivate people, not company values. An organisation's values will inspire, excite, challenge, drive and lift people only if they are aligned with the individual's personal values. We experience all values internally. In fact, we experience 'experience' internally. If the organisation's values do not relate to the individual's personal values, then as far as the individual is concerned the organisation's values do not actually exist.

If people have not identified their own personal values they are unlikely to be able to effectively evaluate the organisation's values or be motivated to align to them and live them at work.

The individual's personal values are important to the organisation for one other reason. We discussed the impact of the global values shift and how people are looking for a greater sense of meaning in their work earlier in this book. Many of us will spend a large percentage of our life at work, and it is important that we work in a manner and a place that allows work to be a meaningful experience. Today, people want their work to give them the opportunity to explore and experience what it means to be a human being.

As much as this may sound like soft New-Age philosophy we can assure you it isn't. From the hundreds of personal values consultations and thousands of conversations with people attending values workshops we have facilitated, we can genuinely say this is a very real issue concerning many New Zealanders and Australians. People want their work to be a fulfilling experience. Simultaneously they genuinely wish to be of value to their employer, and to add value to the organisation, and in return be acknowledged as a valuable team member and contributor to the company's objectives.

Any restrictions people face in their attempt to achieve this sense of contribution and commitment leads to alienation at work, and people leaving the organisation.

We witnessed a rather dramatic example of the benefits that an organisation can reap when it takes into account the personal values of its staff. The company in question ran what it referred to as a 'hunter' sales force, and counted its sales as 'kills'. Salespeople had to achieve a set number of 'kills' per month and failure to do so for two consecutive months led to a serious chat about what it meant to be a hunter. If an individual failed to 'kill' in sufficient quantities over a three-month period, they were dismissed.

Whilst senior management thought this the best approach with which to hit the market, many of their salespeople found that it created an extremely uncomfortable working culture that for many of them conflicted with their personal values.

When we were asked by a senior sales manager to submit a proposal to help employees to increase their 'kills', we politely turned down the opportunity to pitch for the business. The manager's reaction was one of mild indignation, and she asked why we were not interested.

We responded by explaining we wanted to work with organisations that genuinely respected their people, and that we knew the best performance only came as a result of people being aligned with their work. As much as we respected the company's right to select its preferred sales approach, we explained that their current approach contradicted everything we as a company valued and believed in. The manager asked for more details and out of the subsequent conversation it became apparent that the company had been struggling to maintain employees in the sales department and had a turnover of sales people of over 60 per cent.

The manager obviously thought things over because she called into our offices on her way home that night and told us how tiring, stressful and destructive the culture was to work in. This brave woman had apparently resigned after our meeting, and told the senior managers a few home truths about the culture and its impact on her people.

We received another visit from her the following week. She told us she had spent several days at home contemplating things and then returned to work, where she offered to implement some significant changes if the senior management team wanted her back. She was passionate about her people and believed she could work with them to achieve equal revenue targets in what she termed a more humane manner.

She obviously put forward a persuasive argument, and had proven a great loss to her company as she was offered her job back on the spot and within a month had put in place a number of steps to ensure she changed the company culture. We began to work with her and the team to assist them to clarify their own personal values and then determine the relevance and alignment of these values to their role. This proved to be such a success that within three months the senior management team asked to have the same process offered to other departments, including themselves.

It was inspirational to watch this woman help the organisation to break out of its old confrontational culture into an equally efficient but less aggressive one. In the new culture, people were able to accommodate their innate desire to deliver service and sales with the customer's best interests in mind, rather than simply doing whatever it took to reach their sales target.

According to a survey of more than 800 mid-career executives, unhappiness and dissatisfaction are at a 40-year high in the USA (*Washington Post*, 25 August 1996). Over 40 per cent of those surveyed hated their job, either because they did not have roles that were meaningful to them or their values were unaligned with those of the company. Our experiences suggest little has changed between 1996 and now. In *The Fifth Discipline*, Peter Senge notes, 'Without values alignment, staff rarely commit more than is required at the basic minimum level.'

This dissatisfaction is not restricted to the USA; the Compass Group international survey on values reported in *New Wisdom II* found that greater than 40 per cent of people would prefer a different job in a different organisation. In Europe and the Pacific Rim the figure was 60 per cent.

So it appears there is much companies could be doing to ensure their employees have a greater chance of job fulfilment. Interestingly enough, many international surveys show that generally increased financial rewards is not the most sought after form of fulfilment. What people want is for their work to be meaningful.

The word 'meaningful' is, of course, highly subjective, and that is the whole point. People's sense of meaning is a derivative of their personal values. Our personal values make meaning accessible and measurable. People will apply themselves more effectively and energetically to things that they find meaningful.

We are convinced one of the best things a company can provide for its employees is the opportunity to clarify their own values. A company that allows an individual to live their deepest values in the workplace will win the heart and soul of that employee, and this enthusiasm and passion will be shared with all stakeholders. The supposed contradiction between work and play seems to disappear when people realise their own values and are encouraged to bring them into the organisation, for the betterment of all concerned. Without this type of values alignment the best outcome for both individual and organisation will only be mediocre.

The True North approach to clarifying personal values

Though this book is about company values, it is relevant here to mention the work that we do with individuals through our True North personal values workshops. This process is described in detail in a companion book by Michael Henderson, *Finding True North: Discover your values, enrich your life*, which is designed to allow people to understand, determine and apply their own values in their lives. We have run these workshops for a number of years now, and the feedback we have got from attendees has been fantastic. Many people have said that they feel able to bring their whole selves to work as a result of the workshop, that they feel capable of reaching their full potential in all aspects of their lives. The key point for managers contemplating encouraging staff to explore their personal values is that as a result of doing this, in our experience, people give more to their workplace.

In *Flow: the psychology of happiness*, Mihaly Csikszentmihalyi points out that many people habitually underestimate how much they actually enjoy their work. Once people have clarified their personal values and aligned them to their work and the values of their organisation, they discover new and improved ways of conducting themselves at work. We call this the 'True North' experience, because people know where they are going, and they are heading in the 'right' direction (for them). The outcome of an individual who has clarified their personal values and aligned them with the organisation's values can be seen in position 4 of the following diagram.

Relationship between degree of experience of personal values
and alignment with organisation's values

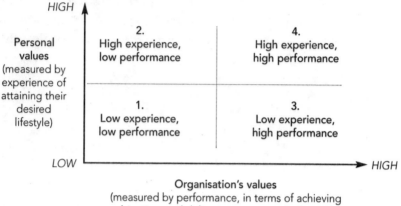

From this diagram we are able to see four varying perspectives of values alignment.

The further up the vertical axis an individual feels they are in relation to achieving their desired lifestyle, the greater the level of values attainment they will be experiencing.

The further to the right on the horizontal axis a company is able to measure the individual's performance, the higher degree of alignment the individual is achieving with the organisation's values.

1. A person who falls within the realms of position 1 is performing at an unsatisfactory level in the eyes of the organisation and has attained little in terms of their own aspirations. They are likely to be sacked or leave of their own accord. This individual doesn't share the organisation's values and doesn't get results.

2. A person at position 2 is attaining what they want in life and their work is part of this process. The organisation, however, does not consider they are contributing enough or at a sufficient level. This person may require feedback-coaching, development training or repositioning. The company's values have little or no impact on this person and they don't get results.

3. A person who fits in position 3 is performing well in the eyes of the company and yet is personally gaining little from the experience. They will perform well only in the short term, and are likely to be highly stressed and dissatisfied, and will probably leave or worse still, become unwell. This individual doesn't share the company values, although they do still get the results.

4. Position 4 is the ideal location for both the organisation and the individual. There is a match between the individual's key values and those of the organisation. This individual is considered to be contributing and is also personally attaining their desires, wants and preferences in life. This is the condition most likely to produce optimum fulfilment and results for all concerned, and in most cases will result in high productivity and profitability. This individual shares the values and gets results.

In summary, if there is a match between an individual's values and those of the company we can expect to see the individual attain more in respect of their desired lifestyle and the organisation will benefit in terms of employee performance.

CHAPTER 14

Embodying values through behaviour

Walking the talk.

—

It is predominately through behaviour that organisations are able to really begin to see, feel and hear their values in action. Linking the organisation's values to behaviours is the key to experiencing the values at work. In other words, it is necessary to 'walk the talk'.

Most organisations with a relatively strong understanding of values are quick to pick up on the task of aligning behaviour to their values. However, some organisations do not think to convert their values into specific preferred behaviours, although these same organisations seem to use job descriptions, performance management systems and key performance indicators to manage behaviour in the business. Too often organisations list their values and fail to make any suggestions on how to actually apply them.

This omission can create all sorts of behavioural interpretations. For example, consider the following four values: family, loyalty, tradition, profit. Many people would be happy to work for an organisation with those values. However, it is not until we see those values as behaviours that we can effectively evaluate them for their relevance and appropriateness. Consider how these values take on quite a different feeling when we recognise them as the likely values of a typical Mafia family, where they might be used to justify extortion, torture and murder.

How values are implemented through behaviour is the true measure of their fit with an organisation's identity and overall purpose.

How to align behaviours to your organisation's values

The ability to identify and link behaviours to a value enables organisations to integrate their values when developing each employee's job description.

The key to aligning behaviours to your organisation's values is the completion of a values and behaviour map. This map, outlined below, enables everyone to link the values of the organisation directly to their individual roles, by identifying behaviours relevant to their role that support the values. Once the process is complete, all the organisation's values will be linked to behaviour, which in turn will be linked to benefits to the organisation, the stakeholders and the individual employees.

A number of our clients have commented that in their previous experience with values projects, this simple and yet apparently obvious part of the values process had been left out. On completing this step, it became immediately apparent to them why earlier attempts to introduce values failed to become part of the culture. As one manager said, 'I can see it's common sense, it just wasn't common practice.'

The example on page 143 shows what a completed behaviour map looks like. It uses the AVI value definition for accountability/ethics, and discusses the preferred behaviour associated with the value.

A similar sheet for the organisation's other values would be completed. All sheets would then be reviewed with the team leader or manager to fine-tune any of the information to better support the individual to align with their role.

Each value should be assessed using a separate table. The entries under the heading 'observable behaviours' should be written in the first person and should describe behaviours that, if other people saw you carry them out, would lead them to conclude you were expressing the value in question. For example, for the value 'service' the entry might read: I am observed listening, smiling, empathising, assisting, problem-solving and questioning. The organisation could also review all employees' charts to assist in determining what support could be provided to further assist people to consider their behaviour.

Another tip for aligning behaviours to the organisation's values is to design each job description using the alignment model outlined in chapter 7. The following table indicates how a completed job description might look for a customer-service representative.

An aligned position description for a customer-service representative	
Role's purpose	To deliver quality service to all our customers
Position (Identity)	Superb telephone customer-service operator
Organisation's values	Quality, performance, people, profit
Key capabilities	Listening, empathy, word-processing skills, product knowledge, costing and sales knowledge, negotiation skills
Specific behaviours	Using customer's name, effective use of open and closed questions, completing order records during the call, confirming the order, arranging freight, speaking with tonal variety and a smile
Context and constraints (environment)	Only deals with software product enquiries and complaints

Using this alignment process the job can be specifically constructed to represent the organisation's values, and to reflect the capabilities and behaviours required in the role.

Typical timeframe for behaviour alignment

How long does it typically take for an organisation to embody its values through behaviours? This varies significantly depending on the circumstances, resources and commitment of the organisation's leaders. Typically, full embodiment of the values in an organisation of over 100

Aligning values and behaviour

VALUE AND MEANING	OBSERVABLE BEHAVIOURS	BENEFITS TO ORGANISATION	BENEFITS TO STAKEHOLDERS	BENEFITS TO SELF
Accountability/Ethics To hold yourself accountable to a code of ethics derived from the values. To address the appropriateness of your behaviour in relation to these values.	I can be observed using the company values when making any decisions in my role. I use the organisation's values card in my pocket or the posters around my work environment whenever I need to confirm that the decision I am about to make is in alignment with the organisation's values. I review my day's work with a colleague in relation to the values.	The benefits to the organisation living the value of accountability / ethics are that we are all empowered to make decisions about the appropriateness of our behaviour on the job, so we require less supervision and monitoring. This saves time, money and energy. The saving of resources and people power can be redirected to other parts of the business requiring extra attention.	People will do what they say they will do. The end result is a successful team producing successful results that are reliable and trustworthy.	I am empowered by being able to determine the appropriateness of my behaviour in relation to the values. This increases my self worth.

people will take 18–24 months. For smaller organisations the timeframe is usually 9–12 months.

The first noticeable collective (as opposed to individual) signs of embodiment typically occur after six months (earlier in smaller organisations). Embodying the values will happen more quickly if individuals are fully aligned to the organisation's values.

CHAPTER 15

Recruiting with values

The employees of the future will be more independent-minded and more mobile, readier to change jobs or careers or even continents. They will join and help shape organisations that reflect their own values.

Robert Jones, *The Big Idea*

—

Having gone to the trouble of establishing their values and committing to doing whatever it takes to ensure the values are lived, organisations often forget to ensure that the personal values of new recruits are aligned with the company's values.

All too often when a new appointment fails to live up to expectations, we hear how the individual just didn't quite fit into the company culture, or that they never really seemed to adopt the company attitude. This is not surprising when appointments are made with little attention to the individual's personal values and their alignment with the organisation.

AES, the decentralised power generation company that operates 90 plants in 13 countries and employs some 40,000 people, featured in the *Harvard Business Review* (Jan–Feb 1999). AES takes a firm stance on values when recruiting staff. The article states, 'AES tends not to pay the highest rate in the industry for its jobs. As one person at the Thames, Connecticut, plant noted, "If you pay the highest, people will fake it in terms of liking the culture and values".'

AES obviously takes its values seriously. It may seem unusual to not try to pay the highest rates to attract the best people, yet from a values perspective this makes total sense. What doesn't make sense is the usual approach of paying top dollar for people who are misaligned with the organisation from a values perspective. In the article, AES CEO Dennis Bakke discusses the organisation's approach to values and recruitment. 'We've made our biggest mistakes in hiring when people have said, "We need someone with such and such expertise," and put cultural fit second. We've been much better off when we've hired people who don't just accept our values but are evangelical about them. I am always amazed at how well some people who have been hired understand what we are doing and how well they manage to spread the news, so to speak.' Bakke continues, 'The whole system would fall apart if we didn't have a lot of people who were passionately excited about our values.'

As discussed earlier, a new generation of people are emerging in the workforce who are looking for a sense of meaning in their work. These are just the type of people who will be willing to sacrifice the top dollars in order to obtain a position in an organisation that has values aligned with their own.

A values-based recruitment process provides an opportunity to identify the alignment of the individual's values at selection time. Examining values provides a more holistic picture of a person, indicating more precisely the potential for a successful employee/employer partnership.

For a number of years we were involved in supporting Blue Star New Zealand Business Supplies Group (now Boise Cascade) in establishing values as a key component of their recruitment process.

Blue Star made a commitment to ensure close attention was paid to how their company values align those of potential recruits. Human Resources General Manager of the group, Peter Leathley, says management had a strong belief in values as a new way of doing business. Blue Star was the parent company of five business units with a combined total of around 1000 employees. Each unit had existed as an individual entity before they were brought together as part of the same company. Most had little experience of staff development and all had undergone a period of significant change and upheaval.

'The upper management team believed in the importance of looking at an individual's skill set not only in terms of what these skills were, but how they were executed in the workplace. That is, how their values contributed to their overall performance. As a selection technique, what you are doing when recruiting using values is looking at the whole person, not just the intellectual and capability aspects, but emotional as well. Knowing what drives, motivates and inspires a person and how this fits with the company's values means the selection decision is far more informed. We use the AVI process along with traditional testing when considering a new appointment at any management level within the organisation. We then look at how their values are aligned to our company values. It allows us to make a more educated decision on how the individual will fit within our culture and ultimately contribute to the business. Far from being wishy-washy, our corporate values include a strong focus on performance and success and we constantly challenge ourselves to live them. If an individual's values are aligned with the company's the business outcomes are far more likely to be positive.'

Leathley says there are clear benefits to the business from using values as a recruitment and staff development tool, which ultimately has the impact of enhancing overall performance. Values for this company are more than a plaque at reception — there is a regular review process for senior management, who must demonstrate they are living up to the corporate values.

'It means we have to make tough calls at times and the extreme example has been the removal of senior people who have not been championing the company values. The point to note here is actions such as this have to also be achieved in alignment with our other values, such as treating people in a fair and respectful way, which is part of our value of treating people as people.'

Leathley says to gain full benefit from a values recruitment programme, there must be a meaningful commitment. 'This process is not for the faint-hearted. To be truly effective you have to be committed and prepared to make hard decisions. It takes time and energy, but it's worth it. For us it has created a new order with higher standards, greater honesty and increased expectations of leadership. Our long-term vision is to live our values in every facet of our business, internally and externally. If we achieve that, we will be a truly fabulous company.'

The benefits Blue Star has noted from this values-based recruitment approach include:

- **Staff retention and attraction.** Candidates see the company as having their needs at heart.

- **Reputation enhancement.** The values approach is improving the company's reputation for developing and valuing its people in the marketplace.

- **Natural attrition.** The personal insights gained from examining alignment with corporate values can result in a realisation for candidates that this is not the job for them and a greater contribution can be made elsewhere.

- **Staff loyalty.** With their personal values taken into consideration, the individual develops a greater sense of the organisation's commitment to its people. This in turn engenders loyalty.

- **Higher standards.** Publicly articulated corporate values raise the performance expectations of all employees, both for themselves and their colleagues. A willingness and freedom to challenge behaviours that are not in alignment with the organisation's values develops.

'The benefits are impressive,' says Leathley. 'Many people, including some of our managers, would not expect such results from something as intangible as values. You have to work for them, but they are possible.'

Blue Star's CEO was also supportive of the values process and was quoted in *Management* magazine in 2000 as saying, 'Because the group needed to go through significant change, we knew we needed good alignment values between our main stakeholders — employees, customers, suppliers, community and shareholders.'

Vodafone New Zealand has adopted a similar approach. If you are excellent at your job, yet you do not live the Vodafone values, you're (in their own language) 'gone'. Their explanation for this approach is that if someone in the business does not fit with their values, then the department, organisation and individual cannot succeed. The renowned Southwestern Airlines in the USA does the same. All individuals are given the opportunity, training, information and support to live their values. Failure to do so results in dismissal.

Recruitment companies on the whole have been slow to pick up on this opportunity to add value to their clients by assisting them in aligning candidates' values to those of the organisation, and vice versa. One director of a recruitment organisation in Auckland told us, when we enquired about their position on values being included as part of the process of successfully placing a candidate, 'We aren't interested in whether the candidate's values are aligned to the job or the organisation. We just place people.' It would seem the global values shift is invisible to them.

An example of a values-based recruitment advertisement that incorporates Burger King's values of pride, passion and performance is reproduced below.

How to recruit to your organisation's values

Successful recruitment with values is enhanced with the use of the only globally validated values inventory, known as the AVI. This values inventory technique is outlined in Appendix 1. Using the AVI enables organisations to:

- identify a person's highest and lowest priority values.

- determine the individual's collective world-view, which is the major focus area for their values.

- identify the likely leadership and thinking preference the individual favours as an expression of their values.

- scan the job description to determine to what extent the values contained in the outline match with those of the various candidates.

- indicate potential levels of stress for an individual based on their perceived ability to live in accordance with their highest priority values.

On a less structured level, managers conducting interviews can ask candidates during the interview about their personal values. This is far more effective than asking the candidate what drives them, as typically candidates will answer the latter question with what they believe the interviewer wishes to hear. Once the manager has an understanding of the candidate's personal values, they could also ask the candidate, 'Given the company's values are W, X, Y and Z, how do you feel you could achieve the objectives of the role in a way that would honour those values without contradicting any of your personal values?'

Managers might also ask whether the candidate has ever faced situations in the workplace where their personal values were undermined or threatened and how they managed the situation. Whichever approach is taken, including an exploration of a candidate's values as part of a job interview is an essential process if a values-based company is to continue to grow and succeed.

CHAPTER 16

Coaching using the values

Coaching behaviour is part of it;
coaching values is all of it.

—

Why we coach to the organisation's values

Coaching to the organisation's values is a simple process, which is easy to learn and enables both managers and team members to work more effectively together to achieve their desired results. In 2001 we watched in interest as an organisation's values disappeared from conscious practice within just three weeks of their official launch. We were invited by the organisation to review their situation and write a report recommending interventions. The organisation had worked hard to ensure their values would 'fly'; however, employee feedback soon revealed where the problem lay. The managers and team leaders had failed to reinforce or support people to align their work-related behaviour with the organisation's values, leaving staff understandably confused and ambivalent about the values that just three weeks earlier they were genuinely excited about. With a bit of work from the managers and patience from the employees, the organisation was able to get back on track quickly through the implementation of a company-wide values-based coaching programme.

There are a number of reasons for offering coaching to help people to align with the organisation's values. Providing managers with the capability and encouragement to coach to the organisation's values is an ideal way of keeping the values and their meaning alive in the day-to-day activities of the company. Coaching helps to keep the values relevant for people by guiding their behaviour and tasks in the greater context of the organisation's culture. People also benefit from reminders about the organisation's values as it encourages them to continue to ensure their own personal values are in alignment with those of their workplace. Organisation's values that are neither talked about, aligned nor have decisions based upon them soon fade out of people's awareness.

Coaching is a user-friendly method for helping people to focus their skills, capabilities, beliefs, values and attitudes towards their work and the organisation. In other words, coaching supports alignment. It can be and often is the crucial factor that helps an organisation to achieve peak performance.

Coaching offers support for people as they try to live the organisation's values. It is quick, timely, inexpensive and effective.

There are many ways of behaving in alignment with a value. Coaching helps people to identify the behaviours that the organisation would prefer them to use in supporting the values.

Background

Good coaching takes planning, skill and practice. It is a vast topic and this book is not the place to provide a detailed review of coaching practice. Instead, we will concentrate on providing an overview of what we have discovered works best when coaching with values within an organisation.

There are many different approaches to coaching, including varying degrees of emphasis placed on strategic objectives (such as visions, missions and goal setting) through to a more holistic emphasis on wellbeing and spirituality, to communication and performance psychology techniques and careerist coaching. We therefore wish to briefly outline the background and development of our chosen coaching approach in order to provide sufficient information to evaluate and compare our technique with other approaches. If you have a preferred coaching technique, it may be possible to enhance it with some elements of our approach.

The Values@work coaching approach

In 1995 we completed research, development and design of a sports-psychology-based coaching programme to help athletes to understand and draw more effectively upon their most under-utilised resource, their own mind. Our process, named 'Razor's Edge', was based on a combination of our experience with neuro-linguistic programming, martial arts and Ayruveda (the ancient Indian approach to life science and wellbeing).

Razor's Edge met with success in the marketplace and we quickly found ourselves working with some of New Zealand's leading sports teams. These included the Auckland Blues rugby team, Auckland Cricket, the Diamonds netball franchise, the All Whites soccer squad, and New Zealand's national touch rugby teams. In addition we worked with some of the nation's top individual athletes in such diverse sporting codes as swimming, squash, sailing, athletics, triathlons and trampoline. We also coached the champion East Coast Bays women's soccer team, where the women applied the Razor's Edge performance methodologies and rose from division three to the women's premier league within three consecutive seasons. These experiences taught us many things about what does and doesn't work in coaching.

Coaching to the organisation's values

A good coach needs a number of personal skills to be effective: session planning, observation and interpretation skills, rapport building, questioning that leads to a learning experience, effective listening and problem-solving among them. With these skills, the following values coaching process works exceptionally well. The process can be divided into three primary key steps: assess, approach, appraise.

Assess

The assessment stage requires the coach to decide on the type of coaching they wish to provide. This typically falls into two categories — positive feedback on behaviour when the employee has acted in accordance with the organisation's values, and corrective feedback when they haven't.

We observed a good example of positive coaching at Burger King, when a crew member was praised for acting in alignment with the company's value of pride when they made an unscheduled cleaning of the men's toilets because they noticed these had become unhygienic. The restaurant manager saw this and provided the crew member with positive feedback.

Another example occurred at Whitcoulls, when a salesperson, discussing a book purchase with a customer, advised them that the book they were about to buy would not provide the information they were looking for. The salesperson could have simply sold the book to the customer, but instead acted in alignment with the company's value of integrity. Though they lost a thirty-dollar sale, they gained a loyal customer who will make repeat purchases. A manager was later heard praising the employee's actions. Both the Burger King and Whitcoulls examples demonstrate managers providing positive feedback to staff to encourage them to repeat behaviour in alignment with the organisations' values.

Alternatively, there may be a requirement for feedback to be provided when an individual's behaviour is not in alignment with the values of the organisation. In these instances there are a series of steps the coach can take. These are discussed in the Approach section on page 157.

Assessing yourself as a coach

Managers can also assess how effective they are as a coach, by using the head, heart and hands model discussed in chapter 11. To recap, successful performance requires understanding and knowledge (head), skills and capability (hands) and attitudes, emotions, beliefs and values (heart). When the three are combined in unison the individual has all the attributes necessary to achieve peak performance as outlined in the diagram on the next page.

Head: what do I know/understand about coaching effectively?

Heart: what do I believe about coaching? How motivated am I?

Hands: what skills do I have as a coach?

Before anyone starts values-based coaching we recommend they assess

The three domains of coaching

themselves in terms of their perceived strengths in the specific head, heart and hands components needed to coach effectively.

If they feel they are deficient in any of these areas, they can seek feedback from fellow coaches on strategies for improvement.

As well as the rather broad approach offered by the head, heart and hands model, many coaches have commented on the immense benefit of utilising Robert Dilts' logical levels model, discussed in chapter 7. An adapted version of this model enables coaches to consider how they can best coach to the values of the organisation and still be in alignment with their own personal values. By learning to integrate each of the levels (purpose, identity, values and beliefs, capabilities, behaviour and environment), the coach empowers themselves to create an all-encompassing approach to their coaching style and ability.

Consider your role as a coach under the logical levels model.

Purpose:	Why am I a coach?
Identity:	A peak performance coach.
Beliefs and values:	What beliefs and values support my coaching? Consider the head, heart and hands model.
Capabilities:	To be able to deliver coaching, I need to be able to . . .

Behaviour: What will others see and hear me doing that shows I am a coach?

Environment: Where and when will I coach?

Dilts' model can also help a coach to clarify the level at which to focus their attention when coaching. To align a person at one level of the model, for example their behaviour, usually requires issues or areas of misalignment at other levels to be addressed. For behavioural issues, for example, it will probably be necessary to consider the levels above (capability, beliefs and values, and identity) and the level below (environment) to locate the root cause of the behaviour. Dilts notes, 'While each level becomes more abstract from the specifics of behaviour and experience, it actually has more and more widespread effect on our behaviour and experience.' This is because in order to solve a problem we need to address it at a different logical level from that at which it is being experienced. 'Each level involves different types of processes and interactions that incorporate and operate on information from the level below it.'

For example, if the Whitcoulls manager had decided to provide feedback to the salesperson using the logical levels model, they would realise that the salesperson's behaviour (recommending a customer not buy an unsuitable book) comes from their capability to deliver customer service, which is important to them (values and beliefs). The manager could therefore mention the values involved, by saying, 'It's great to see you supporting our value of customer service by the advice you gave that customer.'

The model also works for corrective feedback. Imagine the salesperson had sold the book, knowing it was not what the customer really wanted. Instead of focusing on the behaviour, the manager could find out if the salesperson had the capability to find out what the customer wanted; if the answer was no, they would coach at this level. If yes, then they would examine the values and beliefs — what does the salesperson believe about the company value of service and how important is it to them? If need be, they could also examine how the salesperson sees themselves (identity) — as a super salesperson or an awkward teenager struggling with their first job.

The following example of comments that might be made by a sales representative illustrates how different aspects of each level may contribute to an unsatisfactory performance.

Identity:	'Deep down I am not a sales rep.'
Beliefs and values:	'Overcoming objections is too hard. I prefer to just let it be.'
Capability:	'I actually don't know how to handle customers' objections effectively.'
Behaviour:	'I deliberately avoid some customers.'
Environment:	'Our competitors are in all our markets.'

This shows that without taking the top levels into account, traditional training (which typically focuses on capability and behaviour) will not produce long-term results.

Approach

The next step in the coaching process is the approach — i.e. approaching the person being coached and engaging them in dialogue.

It often covers four areas: why, what, how and what if. For example, the coach might say, 'As you know, Murray, one of the organisation's values is customer service. I want to talk with you about some of your recent behaviour with our customers. I have noticed you have ignored customers on several occasions and wondered if there was any reason for this?' (Why).

Murray can now explain his reasons and motivations (What). The coach may then ask him how he sees that behaviour delivering the company value of customer service. If the coach is not satisfied with his response they can then explain why, and take the time to ensure Murray understands their point of view. This may include Murray asking questions about the coach's perspective.

The coach and Murray can then review alternative behaviours that are more aligned to the value (How). Once suitable alternatives have been identified the coach should ensure Murray is willing to attempt the newly identified behaviour, and ask him if he requires any assistance or resource to be able to undertake this new approach. However, if Murray is unable to identify alternative behaviours, the coach can make some suggestions of their own.

It's important to encourage Murray to check that newly identified behaviours are also in full alignment with his personal values (What if?). This can be done simply by asking if the newly identified behaviour is likely to conflict with any of his personal values and if so, in what way. Any conflict identified by these questions needs to be resolved before the behaviours can be implemented.

Finally, a review date should be set to discuss the progress made, and the subject should be thanked for their participation and commitment to the organisation's values.

The coaching enquiry process is summarised below.

Why: Identify the behaviour to be changed and the link to any of the associated company values.

What: Listen to the subject's explanation of the behaviour.

How: Discuss alternative behaviours more aligned with the organisation's values.

What if: Discuss, review and resolve any personal values conflicts likely to arise from the identified behavioural change.

Appraise

The appraisal process is important, because the coach needs to identify how effective their coaching was, and what areas still require further attention and development. The coach could have a checklist of questions to ask themselves regarding the coaching session they have undertaken

Did I ensure Murray was aware of the organisation's values?

Did I know whether the organisation had provided Murray with the opportunity to identify his own values?

Did I describe the performance objectively and specifically?

Did I offer Murray the opportunity to explain his version of events?

Did I have enough facts relating to the situation for Murray to accept the situation as valid and important?

Did I discuss the performance privately rather than in a crowded office?

Did I ensure I was in control of my own emotions?

Did I ensure the coaching session was timely and convenient to Murray?

Did I use an appropriate mix of head, heart and hands elements?

Did I ensure the coaching session met Murray's needs?

Did I ensure it was safe for Murray to communicate openly and honestly with me?

Did I do more than simply provide an opportunity to share information — i.e. was my coaching likely to lead to a change in behaviour?

Did I ensure the coaching session did not have a negative impact on Murray's self-esteem?

A coaching planning form

When these fundamentals of coaching have been understood we can begin to explore some more of the subtleties of coaching by examining a typical coaching planning sheet as outlined below. This example incorporates the Assess, Approach and Appraise phases of coaching. Steps 1–4 comprise the Assess phase, steps 5–9 cover the Approach phase and finally steps 10–11 addresses the Appraise phase.

The example on page 161 should be considered as a guideline only. We encourage you to adopt, change and delete any aspects you require to better suit the needs of your particular culture.

The form on pages 162 and 163 could be used to plan for the coaching session and record your answers

Coaching paradoxes

Ironically, coaching also has some contradictory outcomes that it is useful to be aware of.

- Coaching is initiated more for the coach's benefit than for the person being coached.

- The immediate result of coaching is nearly always reduced performance in the short-term, because it takes a while for the person being coached to assimilate new behaviours, skills or attitudes.

- The success of our coaching is indicated by the performance we get back.

ASSESS

1. **Current situation:**
Sales representative Murray is missing opportunities to inform the customer of additional products that may help them to save time and prevent frustration. A specific example is that he forgot to ask XYZ company if they wished to purchase additional toner for emergency photocopying requirements. Has this been discussed with Murray before? If so, what previous agreement was reached?

2. **Type of feedback:**
Is the feedback required reinforcing or corrective?

3. **The company values affected:**
Service and Professionalism.

4. **Key points to make:**
Consider relating the feedback to the Head, Heart and Hands model, e.g. product knowledge (Head), beliefs about service (Heart), procedures (Hands).

APPROACH

5. **Open the discussion with:**
'I/we value . . .'
'So when I see/hear that . . .'
'I see it as not living the value of . . .'
'Because . . .'

6. **Provide reinforcing feedback:**
'Keep on doing [specific behaviour] . . .

7. **Provide corrective feedback:**
Find out why Murray acted as he did, and what resources he needs to do what's being asked of him next time.

Questions include 'How do you feel about offering our customers this type of support?' and 'Does engaging in this behaviour clash with any of your personal values?'

8. **Agree what actions need to be taken:**
By whom? When? Where?

9. **Ensure the necessary resources are made available, such as support, knowledge and skills training.**

APPRAISE

10. **Schedule a time to meet with Murray to review his progress.**

11. **Conduct an appraisal of the coaching process.**

Coaching record

For:.. Date:....................

---

1. Current situation:

Supportive information:

Coached on this before?   Y   N

Previous agreement

2. Areas affected (what's most important):

❏

❏

❏

❏

❏

---

3. Key points to make:

Head

Hands

Heart

4. Open the discussion with 'I/We value':

'So when I see/hear' . . .
(specific action/behaviour, situation)

'I see it as living/not living the value of' . . .
(affect on what's most important)

'Which is' . . .
(great, unacceptable, brilliant, disappointing, not what we need . . .)

'Because' . . .

---

5. Reinforcing feedback:
Opening statement:
Give a reinforcing message: 'Keep on doing' . . (specific action behaviour) . . .'

6. Corrective feedback:
Opening question:
Find out why they did what they did and what resources they need to do what's being asked of them next time.

Notes:

7. Agreed actions to take:
(Who, when, where . . .)

8. Resources to be made available:
(Support, knowledge, skills . . .)

CHAPTER 17

Values audits

The only way to be sure you are living your values to the fullest possible extent is to complete a values audit. The benefit of a values audit is that it enables you to determine where and how the organisation is best living the values and where there are areas for improvement. Appendix 1 of this book outlines some of the sophisticated values processes that can be incorporated into a comprehensive values audit. However, simpler audits can be conducted quickly and easily by using the sample questionnaire on the next three pages. Alternatively, we have developed an online values audit, an example of which can be viewed at our website **www.valuesatwork.org**

If the company is small, all employees can complete the values audit questionnaire. If not, use a sample cross-section of at least 10 per cent of employees. Audits should be conducted annually, or more frequently if there are noticeable values conflicts. The information generated from the completed questionnaires should be studied to identify key themes and messages that are useful for the organisation to acknowledge and act upon.

Sample questionnaire				
Statement	Yes	Somewhat	No	Don't know
I know the organisation has a clear set of values				
I understand the organisation's values				
The organisation's values have been prioritised				
People can safely challenge decisions they feel are not supporting the organisation's values				
The way my manager behaves reflects the organisation's values				
The area I work in regularly reviews to what degree we are living the organisation's values				
I have had the opportunity to see how my personal values match the organisation's values				
My job is meaningful to me				
We are encouraged to live our personal values				
We are encouraged to live the organisation's values				
We are supported when we live our personal values				
We are supported when we live the organisation's values				
Performance reviews include measuring how individuals are living the organisation's values				
In my area we support each other to live the organisation's values				
I am clear about what the organisation stands for				

Statement	Yes	Somewhat	No	Don't know
Living the organisation's values does not conflict with my personal values				
The organisation stands for something other than just making a profit and increasing shareholders' returns				
The organisation has a clear values set that is based in reality, deliverable and dominates the organisation				
The organisation's values include those values that have been consistent through the organisation's past				
Leadership is aligned with and champions the company values				
The organisation has a values champion				
The values are referred to intentionally and are understood by everyone				
The values each have an aligned and unanimously agreed upon supporting belief				
The values are shared, communicated and understood by all people, who express them in thought, word and action				
All individuals have a clear understanding of their own personal values hierarchy and core values				
The organisation's values are consistent and aligned with the organisation's vision				
The organisation advances in terms of delivering its purpose or mission				
The values are used intentionally to align the organisation's systems and people's behaviours to create an explicit culture				

Statement	Yes	Somewhat	No	Don't know
There is consistency in the beliefs expressed about the organisation's values				
The organisation's people are viewed as the custodians of the company's values, rather than employees				
Values are used to create performance guidelines that are in turn used to inspire and measure performance				
The organisation recruits to the values as much as competency and experience				
Values-based thinking dominates the organisation				
Values form and are recognised as the basis for all decision-making				
The values contribute to a 'we' orientated company culture experience				
The values create loyalty, meaning and understanding				
People feel they are making a difference in their work. Their job feels meaningful to them				
The values are consistently represented in all internal and external communication				
The top 20 per cent of the organisation's client base know what the organisation stands for and experiences the living of the values in that relationship				

CHAPTER 18

Values in practice — interviews with business managers

Consider any great corporation — one that has lasted over
the years — I think you will find that it owes its resiliency
not to its form of organisation or administration and skills,
but to the power of what we call beliefs and the appeal
these beliefs have for its people.

Thomas Watson Sr, founder of IBM

—

Alan Watts
Operations Manager, Burger King New Zealand
Burger King has three values it lives by: pride, passion and performance.
These values were chosen carefully to provide a strategic direction whilst
also offering a cultural emphasis for the vast majority of their employees,
who are predominantly teenagers and young adults.

How do you define values?
They are our preferences. Burger King has determined to do business
in a way that is consistent with our values, which are pride, passion and
performance. We prefer to run our business with pride, passion and
performance. We also prefer to have people in the business who want to
be part of an organisation that operates this way.

Why did Burger King get into values?

We are a people-oriented business — we are all about delivering our promise to our customers and we rely on our 2500 people to ensure that happens. We were looking for a way to support those 2500 people in a manner that went beyond just the systems training that we already offered. We were already involved in performance systems management using the 'balanced scorecard' approach. The theory for the scorecard says, if you can manage the organisational culture you can achieve more than if you operate with a dysfunctional culture. As a relatively young organisation in New Zealand, Burger King's culture had evolved without deliberate planning. We wanted to educate people about how even in a restaurant environment, a deliberate and positive culture can add value to people's experience of working and visiting there and also achieve the desired performance results.

Is it working?

It is. Our results are good. We benchmark well on Burger King International measurement. Of course, we've still got a long way to go, but then there is still a lot to do with the values that we haven't got to yet because of timing and resources.

Is the values process hard for people to understand?

Yes, it is. It requires effective education. Some people just aren't interested, they're just doing a job, they don't want to know. They just want to do the job, get paid and go home. So we have to challenge people to look at that. That's where their personal values play such an important part. We like people to see how it benefits them, how they can get more from their work and put more into their life.

Have there been any major frustrations or challenges with the process?

Only that I'd like to have gone into it in more depth. That's mainly been about resourcing. It all takes time. It's not a quick fix. To do it well, which is of course the only way to do it, you need to budget for it and ensure it receives the right amount of emphasis from a financial, personal energy and time point of view.

How have people responded to the values process?
It's been great because in our business all we need is small incremental improvements within each restaurant to generate great overall results.

It has only done good. Those that have picked up on it have made such a positive difference that they impact and influence the culture more than any people who haven't. Some people have been ambivalent, but that hasn't held us back.

Why some ambivalence?
It is a different way of looking at business and it can take time for people to shift their old habitual viewpoints. In some cases the values we have created did not match with people's personal values. They still tended to see a business as a series of functions only, and wanted to ignore the people element. Also, some people shouldn't be in the business anyway — defining our values has helped some people clarify this for themselves. The end result has been that it's become difficult for them to stay here and feel comfortable, so of course some people have left.

Another reason for ambivalence is that it takes time to get results because we have to resource the process, over a period of two years to date. In our business people operate in short time spans so they are used to almost instant results. Over time we are getting a greater and greater percentage of buy-in as people see the difference it's making.

Have you noted any benefits to people clarifying their own values?
I'm not sure. Of the whole values process that's the area we have yet to really get stuck into. It's the next step for us. I can say it's definitely increased people's awareness of the importance of values.

It has also meant those who have clarified their personal values should be able to put them into practice. It's an important part of the values-education process. It creates greater understanding and buy-in to the process by employees.

It also influences our recruitment process. If the recruiters are aware of a person's values, if these are aligned to the organisation we're a step ahead, it's something they can deliberately look for in interviews. It's no harder to employ people using values than not using them. The benefit is that the people who have been employed by clarifying that their personal values match with those of Burger King have proven to be a better fit (for both parties) and we haven't had to pay any more for the benefit. It also enables managers to be more selective about promotion and recruitment.

What have been the key benefits?
It's created focus, and tied in a greater appreciation for our customer promise for people. It's created an added element to the balanced scorecard. We have needed to develop specific skills in order to deliver the values, which in turn add value to the business in ways we may not have considered. For example, the coaching to values workshop for all our managers, which has been really well received, has offered us value as a business and yet we may not have considered that type of approach in the past.

We're still learning how to get a very specific measurement of the return, however we've undoubtedly had better performance. We had our best financial year ever since commencing the values process and we know the values have had an impact on that. Also, a cultural shift has started to emerge. We're building on our customer service results and overall our financial performance has increased. Our management turnover has declined. There's definitely more of a 'can do' attitude in the business. People are coping more enthusiastically and responding to challenges in a positive way. It's a 'bring it on' attitude. We have had really great responses from people even when we haven't even been able to resource them as much as we'd like.

What advice would you give to any other organisations considering working with values?
Put enough resource into it to make it work and realise it takes time. We run a lean business so we've had to be realistic with funding, planning and supporting people to get the time to work with it. The big thing is being patient — it's exciting stuff so you want to see instant results. It doesn't work like that — people need time. You can't change a business culture over night. In a fast-paced business that's growing, with new people joining, you need to make sure everyone's included in the process. Ideally it becomes part of your induction process. It's important to lock in the senior people in the business. If they're not with the programme it will unravel pretty quickly.

So how do you get buy-in at the senior level?

Firstly, people who come in after the process has started need to be recruited with the values in mind. Secondly, you need to spend time with senior people to help them see the benefits to be gained. It's vital senior people see the values as important to the organisation's strategy.

What would you do differently?

Well, again, I'd increase the commitment and apply as much resource to it as possible because I believe it's got so much to offer. It doesn't happen without commitment and application, especially in an organisation our size. It requires some real effort.

What's worked?

Enlisting a core group of enthusiastic supporters of the process, because one person can't drive it on their own. There's a lot to do and it requires multiple input.

How are the values used for decision-making in the business?

The values link to decision-making still has a way to go to get everyone aligned. A recent example that reflects the use of our values in our decision-making is the decision to cut back offering a breakfast service during the week. Opening early to provide breakfast meant an increase in the time the business had to operate. This in turn was placing additional pressure on some people, which was having an impact on the passion value. Also, the breakfast itself was not of a standard that the crew were proud of offering. The combination of these two facts coupled with the reality that the breakfast menu was not performing as we had hoped meant we needed a change. We have therefore taken on board the feedback and withdrawn the breakfast menu from weekdays whilst we consider how to re-engineer it, so it does match the values.

Another example would be the decision to purchase the Australian Burger King restaurants. Because we are proud of what we've achieved here, we felt we could offer it into another market. We are passionate about Burger King, so although we looked at other opportunities none matched the same level of passion we all felt for Burger King. We also knew that we had the knowledge and commitment to turn the Australian business around and lift its performance.

So has the values process been a worthwhile exercise to go through?
Absolutely! Although we've been at it for two years we have made good progress and there's still so much more we can do. I'm particularly excited about what it has to offer the young people in our company. We have a great opportunity with this process to support people to grow.

Elaine Ford
CEO, Onesource

Onesource is the newly launched brand and organisation combining the resources of the Cogent and Ubix businesses, offering a unique business proposition as a single-source supplier of copiers, faxes, telecommunication and tele-conferencing technology and integration service. These two organisations have had a turbulent past with a number of CEO changes over recent years. The following interview with Elaine Ford was conducted six months after Onesource began the values process.

Why has this organisation undertaken a values process?
It's about achieving that concept of alignment between our people and our organisation. And of course, at the time this organisation started, we weren't aligned, because of the company repositioning and launching Onesource as a new brand in the marketplace. We knew we needed a process to enroll our people and influence the culture and its values to make this work.

Although I understand that of course you can't just tell people to 'be aligned', you'd like to be able to just say, 'OK, let's all get lined up in the same direction and off we go.' There needed to be a programme to guide us through this and help people to understand what was happening and why, which is the 'head' part of the values process.

Using the head, heart, hands model lets people know that we will support them to develop the capabilities (hands) to cope with the change and not to be threatened by it.

However the key part is the heart, which means they actually want to move with these changes. They need to work out for themselves that if this process is perceived to be damaging in any way for them personally, and they don't want to be part of it, they can more comfortably go their own way. Being unaligned doesn't work for anyone, individuals or the organisation.

I've noticed in our discussions you regularly refer to the head, heart and hands values model. What is it about the model that appeals to you?
It just makes it so simple to explain to people how values work and why they're so important.

What we do with values has to transcend the workplace and it has to refer to the person's whole life, because it helps people to access the power of values and to easily buy into the process. The model isn't just about work — it has to do with everything we do in life.

How easy has it been to get management buy-in to the process?
It's been nearly impossible. People here felt threatened by yet another new initiative. Given the past this organisation has experienced, they find it hard to trust that we would be doing the values process as much for them as for the business. In the past they've felt it was dangerous to show their true colours, so now they don't trust that this is a personal development opportunity for them. These are people who tend to say 'what's in it for me?' by which they specifically mean money. I'm thinking at a different level of what's in it for them and I'm thinking, 'but I'm giving you a lot here. There's the world in it for you, it could literally change your life for the better.' Yet there was still distrust of our motives and people felt very threatened by what they perceived as 'soft stuff', which flatly they didn't want to know about.

So there was a mismatch there, which is why the alignment process is important.

It also takes a certain amount of personal strength and awareness to actually be receptive to this sort of concept in personal growth. This organisation has traditionally been very macho, and that means this isn't the done thing for some men.

How have those who have been sceptical coped? Have you seen any changes or have there been any surprises?
I've absolutely steamrolled through this till they've done their personal values using the AVI (see Appendix 2) and they have received some guidance on how to interpret their personal values inventories. Then if they want to discuss their reasons for opting out we can have an informed discussion with them.

I've found that almost without exception, those who were very sceptical and resistant, who we insisted participate in the process, have ended up saying, 'Oh, that was actually quite useful, I needed that, it's given me lots to think about.' We've had lots of sceptics converted.

Now that most of the managers have completed the AVI feedback, I think we'll see a real commitment and buy-in to taking values wider within the organisation at the next management meeting.

It could be coincidental, but since we've started this we've had a real swing across to accepting Onesource as a brand and as a business concept. Now I can't tell you specifically how it's been attributed to the values process, but we're swinging faster than we were expecting.

What's driving that?
I like to think it's mainly coming from the executive level. I think some of the work you've done with our executive team has been very positive. It's one of the things people are regularly commenting on either directly to me or via a third party, that they see we have an executive team that is aligned. They see we're passionate about the vision, to the point that the vision would continue even if I weren't here, which is great, as obviously that's an important part of my role.

So we're certainly seeing results with the executive team. I never find myself reminding the executive team of the direction we are taking. They are totally on board. I recently managed to negotiate with Hanover, our owners, for performance bonuses for the team and someone commented, 'Wow, with that in place they would crawl over broken glass to get results.' I replied, 'But they would anyway, without this. This isn't an incentive, it's a reward.' It's like that here now. It's like we are all protecting the vision. It's very exciting. We just need to get this happening at a branch manager level.

What do you perceive as the challenges in this type of work in an organisation?
It's taken real drive from me. I've not been in a position before to choose what tools or approach I use in an organisation. So this values approach has been especially important to me because I've got total belief in it.

I think it wouldn't actually happen without CEO commitment. It took me a long time to get it started from the time we first met, because at that stage we didn't have executive team buy-in to the concept. This was important to achieve otherwise we couldn't get going. To start with we had surges, and the surges had to constantly come from me. Now we have executive members who have clarified their own values and are on board, so the surges are now coming from them too. So it certainly needs leading from the top.

What other challenges have there been?
We've got 500 people in the business to involve, so there's the whole economics of how much do we spend, and does it need to be a hierarchical cascade. The bridge I haven't crossed yet is how important is the compliance or understanding and believing in the value of doing this, because I suppose I feel deep down that if anyone isn't being honest with themselves or us, it's going to show. I'm not sure what we are going to do if we get people in key roles who don't respond. Actually, I'm not sure that I want them in key roles.

Some of our other clients have reached a decision that it just becomes non-negotiable. So you may be superb at your job but if you're not living the organisation's values in alignment with your own, you're gone!
Well I think that's what's going to happen here too, which is why it's so important that people clarify their own values because otherwise I am not being fair to them. I think we are really giving them some whole life tools. A lot of the people in this business don't have a wide-ranging life experience, this could be incredible wealth we are giving them, even if they don't know that now.

If that's happening for them, it has to come back round to us. Sooner or later they will see how and why it's happening and that engenders all those things they want, like trust and loyalty, all those goals can come as a result of the fact they are also living their own values at work. It's the only way we can create those types of experiences — together, not by management being solely responsible for their delivery.

What are your expectations of the values process?
When you've got that alignment it's like an aerodynamic effect. So we'll go faster, the ride will be smoother and our performance will improve.

Given your exposure to the process and, I believe, heartfelt connection with the process, what advice would you have for other organisations, or more specifically leaders, that are just beginning to look at this and consider it as an option?

It's not just a human resources tool you can buy and pay for people to come in and do it for you. It requires internal ownership from the top. I mean, I use this personally, among other tools.

Because it is about the values we live, it's fundamental to all levels of the organisation. So I think the advice I would give is to do what we did — start at the top with the senior executives and see what happens. If you don't get people at that level, I don't think you can get it through.

Also, what worked for us was presenting values education sessions at our national sales conference, to get a groundswell of interest. I used that groundswell of interest to gain momentum for the process. Have a goal in mind and you can push on through. We expect the process to take up to two years, as it's such a deep and fundamental issue.

The values process is also a philosophy on business, and the way people here have interpreted it, they have a real excitement about it and a twinkle in their eyes. People are walking around saying, 'I had all those low priority things cluttering me and now I can just let them go.'

How useful and credible has the leadership values inventory proven to be in your opinion?

I think you can predict behaviours and events in the business with it, if you've done it pervasively enough.

It's enabled me to get a deeper understanding of where people are coming from and why they are behaving in a certain way, to the extent I am able to almost predict how they are likely to respond. This process differs from most things like this because normally you are boxed as a specific type. The values inventory enables you to understand how you can change if you wish to, which is often what we need, because it's going to require individuals in the organisation to change in order for the whole organisation to change.

Have you seen the benefit in people having the opportunity to clarify their own personal values as part of the process?

I've seen it with the executive team, and it's starting to filter through from the branch managers. There's still a powerful application of this process — which we are not using enough in the business — and that is for more consultation with one another, where we just talk about what's happening in the business and how this relates to values.

It also helps us understand the underlying drivers of our behaviours rather than just trying to fix the behaviours at a surface level, which often doesn't work or is short term.

It also helps people understand for themselves what changes they want to make, which can then transcend into things such as effective training programmes or individual development plans. Too often people see development plans as being 'I want a promotion — how do I get it?' or 'I need more money,' or 'I need to get a new computer.'

Instead of just limiting development to these types of areas we can expand people's thinking to include, 'I'd like to deal with some of the details in my values inventories.'

This will eventually become part of the culture, where traditional skills and knowledge development is complemented by some worthy personal development.

What's your perception on the role work has for us in our life as individuals?
It's a holistic whole. On the one hand you hear people say they're passionate about their work and yet often their behaviour says the opposite. We want to move beyond that. I like your concept of peak performance as a result of peak experience. Somehow it has to be right. When people are valuing what they experience, and what they are doing as fulfilling in their lives, you have that alignment for everyone, don't you? Everyone wins, and that's what we want.

Ian Draper
CEO, Whitcoulls
Whitcoulls places a significant emphasis on values; firstly to ensure they maintain their traditional association with the New Zealand market, and secondly to maintain and grow the degree of values alignment with new parent company WH Smith.

How do you feel about values having a role to play in the modern business environment?

I'm a great believer in values. It may be a modern business world and yet it's all about those traditional values, you know the type of thing — your word is your bond, be true to your word, that type of thing. My father brought me up on these type of values and made sure they had a place in his own business.

Specifically, what role do values have in organisations?

The most important thing is that the value creates a certain type of culture, to attract the right people and repel those who don't fit. We tried to create a culture where people enjoy themselves, where values like integrity are respected and it's not seen as being a political thing or even as a threatening thing. People spend a large part of their lives at work and it's important that it's a positive experience. Values can do that. It doesn't have to be complicated. I often say 'a camel is a racehorse designed by a committee'. So you want the values to feel natural not enforced.

As a business we can't afford to pay top dollars for people so we want to compensate by creating a positive environment that's great to work in and supports people's overall lifestyle.

Do you think many organisations are starting to think of values in that way?

I think many people in business out there still think values are soft, that they have no connection to profit, performance and results. Yet at the same time these same people will say that their people are their greatest asset. So there is probably still a way to go to resolve that type of confused thinking.

What do you say to people who ask what values have to do with making a profit?

The only way you ever achieve profit is through your people. We have 1200 employees, all of whom are the face of Whitcoulls. If they are not aligned with who we are and what we stand for, then by definition the fundamentals of our business are not delivered. It's just common sense.

Why did Whitcoulls get into values?

The leadership team wanted the organisation to genuinely be part of the community. We have a special relationship with the New Zealand public, we have been around for a long time. There's a history there and we are trusted. We wanted to continue that relationship and trust.

People here really care about other people and you stand out if you don't. In fact, people get ejected from this culture when their personal values mismatch with the organisation's. It's not about their capability, it's about their attitude and their expectations. They know they don't fit because they feel uncomfortable here doing what we do and how we do it.

I'd hate to think anyone ever left here without knowing why they left because their own values weren't clear to them.

So values seem like a natural way of supporting our people and culture to continue to grow with the aspects of the business that the community relate to. WH Smith, our new owners, refer to the culture of their business as their business DNA. I like that analogy. It's true, it's just like that. Their culture is driven by their values.

Do the organisation's values transfer to the shop floor?

About 60 per cent of the people would say yes. Some people are attendees rather than participants. We can use our organisation's values for the rationale for our decisions and encourage people to think about the values for all their important decision-making. We ensure in our policies that we are representing and communicating our values. We ask our people to go the extra mile and often the extra mile is a lonely place, so the more people feel they are in an environment that genuinely supports that attitude the better.

Can you give me an example of how the values are transferred into day-to-day activity on the shop floor?

Sure, that's easy. Let's take our people value, which is all about treating people the way you'd like to be treated. This value means it doesn't serve us or the customer to have the customer purchase a book, for example, and then get home and remember they forgot to buy some wrapping paper and tape to wrap it as a gift. So our people are encouraged to take enough interest in other people to ask something like, 'I see you have a birthday card here, do you need some wrapping paper and tape for that too?'

Isn't that just like 'Would you like fries with that?'
It could seem like that if we weren't genuine about what we were doing. Our people genuinely want to help people with their purchases. For example, you may have seen our 'staff pick' approach with books.

Is that where staff choose their favourite reads and write a small card to sit with the book on the shelf for customers to read and consider?
Yes, that's it. That came about because people in the stores were always being asked for recommendations, so they wanted to make these thoughts more readily available for customers. The process also reflects our company value of 'integrity', which is all about only saying and doing what we mean. That means in order to write one of those recommended read cards you have to really have enjoyed the book and be able to explain why.

The same applies with our 'guaranteed read' approach. This happens when our senior managers all think that a particular book is absolutely awesome and will add value to any reader's experience. The guarantee is, if you buy the book and you don't like it we'll give you your money back. Again, we only recommend books we have that degree of belief in.

Have you encountered any scepticism towards the values process from people within the business?
No, people seem to be right on board with it all. It's the way they want the business to be. We don't always make decisions people like, but we do always base them on our values. We've had great buy-in from the leaders within the business, which is important. People depend on their leader's buy-in to the values and work with them to deliver consistency around our values for everyone, including our suppliers.

Tell me about what you have done to support individuals in the business to clarify their own values?
We have supported all our managers to clarify their personal values and determine to what extent they're aligned with the organisation's. People come away feeling they're in the right place. They appreciate the oppor-

tunity, they're grateful for the time to think and challenge themselves. It makes people feel good about themselves and the company.

It's been well received because it's not just another course to simply improve their productivity. It helps them recognise the company is a good fit for them. They realise things like it's a fun job with good people with educational, entertaining products. This also fits with our company value of community, and lots of people are able to find alignment because they can contribute even in a small way to the greater community. A lot of our people want to do this, based on their own personal values.

How important do you believe it is to clarify personal values in relation to our work?
I absolutely endorse clarifying personal values. It's absolutely part of the process.

Any advice for organisations considering getting into values?
Do it! It's the right thing to do. I can't keep people on a dollar basis only, but if I create an environment that they enjoy they will stay. That's why values are so beneficial. It's about adding and building on the value of their work. So when a candidate for a job with us asks about hourly pay rates in relation to other opportunities they may be looking at, we ask them to think about those other organisations and consider which company would enable them to take time off work to watch their son's egg-and-spoon race at school during work hours. We explain we are about people and about community and ask if that's important to them.

The other piece of advice I have is the one thing I've learnt about the values process — just as the Mainland cheese TV advertisement proclaims — is that good things take time, and values are a good thing for people and the organisation.

Measuring your organisation's values with 'A Values Inventory'

The ancient Chinese character for 'business'
is translated as 'meaning'.

Measuring the success of implementing values in an organisation is often subjective and anecdotal. For people wanting more specific measurement of results, a values measurement process has been developed, based on over 30 years of values research.

The research started with the work of Paulo Freire and Ivan Illich in Brazil, who used energy-laden words to raise people's awareness of their social situation and to increase their level of literacy. Brian Hall, working alongside them, realised these energy-laden words were indicators of people's value priorities. The concept of a values inventory was born.

Brian Hall and Benjamin Tonna collaborated to develop the Hall–Tonna Inventory of Values. In 1988, Colins and Chippendale brought the inventory to Australia. Since then, a system of values analysis has been developed and refined, using the latest research into the brain's functioning and people's thinking processes. The inventory definitions are reproduced in Appendix 2.

Validation

In 1983 the Hall–Tonna values inventory was subjected to a series of validation procedures. The set of 125 values (listed in Appendix 2) were given standardised definitions and a cross-disciplinary and cross-cultural team compared each of the value selectors to the value definitions that stand behind them. Through this process the value statements and definitions were further reviewed and modified. The questionnaire was field-tested on 3000 people, and its reliability and validity was assessed and confirmed by Behaviordyne, USA.

In 1994, Colins and Chippendale developed a new questionnaire based on William Glasser's control-theory principles. The new questionnaire uses language more familiar to the Australasian culture. Validity was assessed by comparing the profiles of people who had completed the original questionnaire, with their profiles after completing the new questionnaire, which continues to be used today.

The values inventory tools enable a measurable and scientifically validated inventory to be taken of a company's values, individual values, group and team values and the values contained in company literature, brochures and job descriptions. From this information, a strategy can be designed to create the most effective and congruent values to align your company.

The values inventory is not some intellectual academic values system, or a way of imposing a values framework on individuals and teams. The 125 values were not constructed through some abstract intellectual exercise but were catalogued through listening to what is important to people of different races and cultures around the globe over many years. The inventory was established by providing people with a questionnaire that asks them to repeatedly choose between the values. The process helps them to create a personal inventory and a hierarchy of their values. The methodology used to analyse the answers to the questionnaire is too complex to reproduce in this book (as answers to some questions affect the analysis of other answers). The questionnaire can be viewed at www.valuesatwork.org

One of the benefits of this approach is that it gives people a language to express to others (and themselves) what is really important to them. We have found that people are often passionate about certain values without being able to articulate them or even in some cases put them into action. Chippendale notes, 'We find Minessence is a very important value to many people but, prior to doing the questionnaire, they are not conscious of how that value impacts on their life choices.' (Minessence is a value that relates to taking complex technologies or ideas and making them simple for the benefit of others.)

Values clusters

The 125 values fall into eight distinct and natural groups known as clusters. The eight clusters are:

- Self preservation
- Security
- Belonging
- Organisation
- Service
- New order
- Wisdom
- Transcendence

Each cluster has a set number of values belonging to it and depending on how many and how often an individual or group selects these values in the questionnaire, the values inventory will indicate what percentage of the individual's overall attention and mental energy is typically directed into each cluster by the priority on it. The clusters are shown in the diagram below.

The values balance

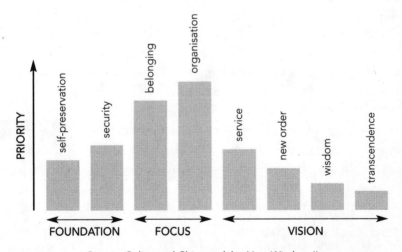

Source: Colins and Chippendale, *New Wisdom II*

On first impression many people comment that these values clusters look remarkably similar to Maslow's hierarchy of needs, as they do in fact share similar names. The significant difference is that the values inventory does not presume there is a hierarchy amongst the cluster, with, for example, self preservation sitting at the bottom and transcendence at the top. From the AVI perspective, what is important for one person may not be for another. So unlike Maslow's hierarchy, which suggests we can only self-actualise once we have taken care of our basic needs such as food, warmth and shelter, the values inventory acknowledges that some people in the world self-actualise no matter where they are on Maslow's hierachy. Good examples of this are Asia's saddhus, yogis and American shaman. The values inventory does not suggest that living one set of values is 'better' than another.

It does suggest, however, that knowing what your values are and what is most important to you is better than not knowing. That way, you can better achieve your objectives and live your life deliberately on your own terms.

Value priorities

A values inventory also indicates the level of priority we allocate to each value. Each of the 125 values can be selected up to five times within the questionnaire, to satisfy each of the four underlying basic human needs: fun, love, freedom and mastery.

Determining our levels of priority enables us as individuals, groups and organisations to evaluate our values to determine if the amount of attention we place on one area is too much, just right or too little.

Goals and means values

By analysing values clusters we can see which values have been prioritised and to what extent. We can also see how much energy is directed into each cluster, and which of the values selected are goal values and which are means values.

Goal values are those that are an end in themselves. In other words, they are valued for the satisfaction of experiencing them. For example, the values Family and Self-worth, which fall into the Belonging cluster, are goal values. The other values in that cluster are means values — that is, they are the means by which the goal values can be achieved. So, the four means values of Social Affirmation, Rights/Respect, Control/Order/Discipline and Endurance/Patience are the means to achieving the goals of experiencing Self-worth and a sense of Family.

In the same way, if an athlete has identified a goal of winning a medal at the Olympics, he or she will have to focus on the means to achieving that goal. This will probably include strength and endurance training, technique development, dietary and sleeping considerations and, of course, coaching and competition. As individuals, we can identify what is most important to us in work or life, and then work out what we need to pay attention to in order to move towards experiencing those goals.

When we begin to consider our values in this manner we begin to understand the strategic nature of our values. This strategic nature can be further understood by discovering how values relate to time. Values fall into three time-based areas of Foundation (past), Focus (present) and Vision (future).

Foundation values are values that need to be taken care of on a daily basis. They are also values we tend to put energy into when we are stressed.

Focus values relate to the way you see the world today. They are the values you would normally put most of your energy into. These values also indicate our beliefs and assumptions about life in general.

Vision values relate to how you believe your world can be in the future. Although not yet experienced, these are the future values you aspire to and the ones that will motivate you.

Measuring an organisation's values

The AVI process can be used for evaluating and enhancing the following areas:

- Recruitment and job description parameters

- Leadership development

- Personal development

- Team development and alignment

- Departmental and company strategic planning

- Cultural values analysis

- Customer and client values alignment research

- Strengthening relationships

- Company and group culture mapping

Values scan

The second significant development in values measurement is the values scan. This process enables a document such as a organisation's annual report, a job description, a mission or vision statement, proposals, marketing briefs, training manuals and so on to be scanned for the presence and frequency of the 125 values.

This is a very useful and exciting development as it provides a means of auditing any written communication for the alignment of values represented in the document with those values the organisation stands for. For example, we have worked with a power company to determine if its proposed organisational values are suitably aligned with its strategic vision. The organisation approached us when they realised that unaligned values would jeopardise their success of achieving their vision.

A values scan also enables an individual to specifically and accurately compare their own values (using the AVI) with those of their job description (using the values scan). From this analysis people can determine to what extent they are aligned with the values of their position and what can be done to create greater values alignment in areas where this is currently lacking. A values scan can also be used as part of the recruitment process, to compare the values required in a position with the values displayed by the individual.

Culture field maps

Paul Chippendale has developed a means of capturing the high priority values of a culture and determining the most likely focus of energy resulting from such a values set. This enables us to gain a picture of what an organisation's culture looks like from a values perspective. These reports are known as culture field maps and have evolved out of Chippendale's study of the work of Paul Tosey and Peter Smith.

Tosey and Smith have developed a means of measuring an organisation's energy investment. Their theory provides a way of looking at organisations (specifically their structure and order) as conceptual controls. In other words, they believe it is the ideas and thinking within the organisation that control the business, rather than managers with authority.

Using a culture field map, organisational order can be seen as being generated by fields. The term 'field' is borrowed from quantum science; it means an area of activity and any apparent random acts observed within that area. This activity and apparent randomness is not unlike individual behaviour in an organisation. It is only when one understands the larger scope of intention that the individual movement and motives become more measurable and meaningful. For example, the frenzied activity of a call centre may look random to an outside observer without understanding the purpose behind the phone calls.

One of the most powerful fields in an organisation is shared meaning. In *Leadership and the New Science*, Margaret Wheatley says, 'In the field view of organisations, clarity about values or vision is important, but it's only half the task. Creating the field through the dissemination of those ideas is essential. The field must reach all comers of the organisation, involve everyone and be available everywhere . . . we must fill all the spaces with the messages we care about. If we do that, fields develop — and with them their wondrous capacity to bring energy into form.'

A culture field map consists of eight energy field designations, as follows:

Integration/Insight
The area of Integration/Insight consists of values that relate to the systems and processes that link the parts to the whole. This enables synergy and structural tension to operate within an organisation. The ability to recognise, monitor, evaluate and adjust systems falls into this category. Values relevant to this area include Synergy, Adaptability, Flexibility, Evaluation and Co-operation.

Inspiration/Spirit
The visionary values of the organisation and its culture are captured

within the category of Inspiration/Spirit. These values foster the ideals of the organisation, indicating what it strives for, the nature of its service, and the overall spirit it wishes to engender. Values relevant to this area include Service, Vocation, Faith, Risk, Vision, Pioneerism and Generosity.

Leisure/Pleasure

The values within the Leisure/Pleasure area are all about ensuring there is a playful element within the culture. This is often required to balance a stress-inducing culture or an excessively driven work ethic. Values from this area include Relaxation, Simplicity, Play and Expressiveness.

Existence/Basic competency

The values represented in the Existence/Basic Competency area are apparent when an organisation is focused on having the necessary resources to do things well. An organisation that has a focus on safety, survival and security will usually have a significant number of values highlighted in this area. Values from this area include Profit, Efficiency, Competence, Confidence and Security.

Activity/Action

The values in the Activity/Action area are all about creating a focus on success and achievement. The emphasis is on values that energise doing, being excellent and getting results. Values from this area include Achievement, Competition, Productivity and Growth.

Control/Order

The Control/Order values are very much about how things should be done. Organisations that prioritise these values maintain control through rules, traditions, ownership and obedience. Companies with a traditional and hierarchical structure tend to favour such values. Values from this area include Administration, Control, Discipline, Obedience, Duty, Law, Tradition, Management, Hierarchy, Membership and Institution.

Community/Heart

The values associated with the Community/Heart area of culture emphasise human interaction and relationships. An organisation that has any people awareness at all will include values associated with this area. Values from this area include Empathy, Support, Rights and Respect, Friendship, Belonging, Discernment and Community.

Meaning/Truth

The values associated with the area of Meaning/Truth are predominantly about successful communication. Although many companies place a high priority on this area as an espoused value cluster, they often fail to deliver on it. Values from this area include Being Self, Word, Communication, Information, Sharing, Listening and Trust.

Each of the 125 values within the AVI falls into one of these eight energy field designations. When a company's values are placed into a culture field map, we get an overall picture of the culture likely to emanate from its values. If we then create a culture field map for a position description and compare that to the company field map, we can see to what extent the position is in alignment with the organisation's culture. Both the culture and position maps can also be compared with an individual's culture field map. These maps make values alignment so much easier as we can specifically identify parts of the organisation that are naturally aligned and also see which areas or people may require further support. Finally, culture field maps can also be used to assist in the integration of two companies or departments with different culture as is the case in restructuring, takeovers and acquisitions.

Examples of culture field maps are set out on page 192. The degree to which the grey area approaches the perimeter of the map indicates the degree of importance placed on that energy field. For example, Company A places a high priority on Community/Heart, whereas Company B expends more energy in the areas of Integration/Insight and Activity/Action.

If Companies A and B were to merge, an analysis of their culture field maps would help them to understand the other's culture. They could then see if it was possible to accommodate both companies' preferences in order to minimise negative impact on both staff and the organisation.

Sample culture field maps

Company A

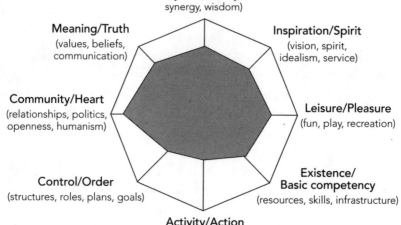

Integration/Insight
(system, totality, synergy, wisdom)

Meaning/Truth
(values, beliefs, communication)

Inspiration/Spirit
(vision, spirit, idealism, service)

Community/Heart
(relationships, politics, openness, humanism)

Leisure/Pleasure
(fun, play, recreation)

Control/Order
(structures, roles, plans, goals)

**Existence/
Basic competency**
(resources, skills, infrastructure)

Activity/Action
(excellence, enthusiasm, results orientation)

Company B

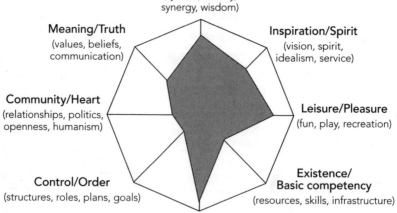

Integration/Insight
(system, totality, synergy, wisdom)

Meaning/Truth
(values, beliefs, communication)

Inspiration/Spirit
(vision, spirit, idealism, service)

Community/Heart
(relationships, politics, openness, humanism)

Leisure/Pleasure
(fun, play, recreation)

Control/Order
(structures, roles, plans, goals)

**Existence/
Basic competency**
(resources, skills, infrastructure)

Activity/Action
(excellence, enthusiasm, results orientation)

The 125 AVI values definitions

The AVI list of values discussed in detail in Appendix 1 is reproduced in full below.

You may find words in the list that you have not come across before, such as 'ecority' or 'minessence'. These are in fact newly developed words to capture concepts people value but did not have a specific word for. For example, 'minessence' means 'to miniaturise and simplify complex technology into concrete and practical applications for the purpose of creatively impacting on the world-view of the user'.

Accountability/Ethics
To hold yourself and others accountable to a code of ethics derived from your values. To address the appropriateness of your behaviour in relation to your values.

Achievement
To accomplish something noteworthy and admirable in your work, education, or your life in general.

Adaptability/Flexibility
To adjust yourself readily to changing conditions and to remain flexible during ongoing processes.

Administration/Control
To be in command. To exercise specific administrative functions and tasks in a business or institution, such as finance or recruitment.

Affection

To express fondness or devotion through physical touch.

Art/Beauty

To experience intense mental pleasure through observing that which is aesthetically appealing in either natural or human creations.

Assertion/Directedness

To put yourself forward boldly regarding a personal line of thought or action.

Being liked

To experience friendly feelings from your peers.

Being self

The desire to know the truth about yourself and the world around you. This includes seeking an objective awareness of your personal strengths and limitations. The desire be yourself in all situations.

Care/Nurture

To be physically and emotionally supported by family and friends throughout your life and to value the same from others.

Collaboration/Subsidiarity

Interdependent co-operation with all levels of management, ensuring full and appropriate delegation of responsibility takes place.

Communications/Information

The effective and efficient flow of ideas and factual information to persons in all or part of an organisation.

Community/Personalist

To have sufficient depth and quality of commitment to a group, its members and its purpose, so that independent creativity and interdependent cooperation will be maximised simultaneously.

Community/Supportive
The desire to have, or to create, a group of peers for the purpose of ongoing mutual support and the creative enhancement of each other.

Competence/Confidence
To experience the realistic and objective confidence that you have the skills to achieve in the world of work and to feel that your skills are making a positive contribution.

Competition
To be energised by a sense of rivalry, to be first or most respected in a given arena, e.g. sports, education or work.

Congruence
To experience and express your feelings and thoughts in such a way that what you communicate externally to others is the same as what you experience internally.

Construction/New order
To initiate and to develop a new form of institution or organisation for the purpose of creatively enhancing society.

Contemplation/Asceticism
The self-discipline and art of meditative reflection that prepares you for intimacy with others and that gives you a sense of being part of something bigger than yourself.

Control/Order/Discipline
To control people and/or things according to prescribed rules so as to maintain the accepted level of discipline and order.

Convivial technology
The application of technology for the benefit of both humanity and the planet.

Co-operation/Complementarity
To work cooperatively in a group so that the unique skills and qualities of one individual supplement, support and enhance the skills and qualities of the others in the group.

Corporation/New order
The innovative design of new organisational or institutional forms which, if implemented, would creatively enhance society.

Courtesy/Hospitality
To treat others, and be treated by them, in a polite, respectful, friendly and generous manner.

Creativity/Ideation
Original thought and expression that converts, for the first time, new ideas, images or concepts into practical and concrete forms.

Criteria/Rationality
To think logically and reasonably using a formal framework for analysis. To exercise reason before emotion.

Decision/Initiation
To take personal responsibility for beginning a creative course of action. To act on your conscience without external prompting.

Design/Pattern/Order
To have an awareness of the natural arrangement of things. To use this awareness to create new arrangements through the application of the arts, ideas or technology; e.g. architecture.

Detachment/Solitude
Regular discipline of non-attachment to external things that leads to the potential to live more fully.

Detachment/Transcendence
Spiritual discipline and detachment so as to experience a global and visionary perspective through a feeling of being in touch with some ultimate source of wisdom.

Dexterity/Co-ordination
Sufficient harmonious interaction of your mental and physical functions to perform basic instrumental tasks, e.g. following a knitting pattern to knit a jersey.

Discernment/Communal
To make consensus decisions, relative to long-term planning for a group or organisation, through prayerful reflection and honest interaction.

Duty/Obligation
To closely follow established customs and regulations out of dedication to your peers and a sense of responsibility to institutional codes.

Economics/Profit
To accumulate physical wealth in order to be secure and respected.

Economics/Success
To attain favourable and prosperous financial results in business through effective control and efficient management of resources.

Ecority/Aesthetics
The personal, organisational or conceptual influence to enable persons to take authority for the created order of the world and to enhance its beauty and balance through creative technology in ways that have worldwide influence.

Education/Certification
To value completing a formally prescribed course of learning and to receive a certificate of accomplishment.

Education/Knowledge/Insight

To experience ongoing learning as a means of gaining new facts, truths and principles, motivated by the reward of a new understanding gained through insight. To enjoy the 'A ha' experience of learning.

Efficiency/Planning

To plan processes and activities which, when implemented, will make the best possible use of available resources.

Empathy

The ability of being able to see things from other people's point of view.

Endurance/Patience

To bear difficult and painful experiences, situations or persons with calm, stability and perseverance.

Equality/Liberation

To experience yourself as having the same value and rights as all other human beings in such a way that you are set free to be yourself and to free others to be themselves.

Equilibrium

To maintain a peaceful social environment by averting upsets and avoiding conflicts.

Equity/Rights

To have an awareness of the moral and ethical claim of all persons (including yourself) to legal, social and economic equality and fairness plus a personal commitment to advocate this claim.

Evaluation/Self-system

To appreciate an objective appraisal of yourself. To be open to what others reflect back to you as being necessary for self-awareness and personal growth.

Expressiveness/Freedom/Joy

To share your feelings and fantasies so openly and spontaneously that others feel free to do the same.

Faith/Risk/Vision

To commit to a cause, or to champion a way of life, even if it may mean putting your lifestyle at risk.

Family/Belonging

To devote yourself to, or be concerned about, your family. To belong to and be accepted by your family. To have a place to call home.

Fantasy/Play

To experience your personal worth through unrestrained imagination and personal amusement.

Food/Warmth/Shelter

To have adequate physical nourishment, warmth and comfort and a place of refuge from the elements. To be protected from the natural elements.

Friendship/Belonging

To have friends to share things with on a day-to-day basis.

Function/Physical

To be able to perform minimal manipulations of your body to care for yourself. To be concerned about the body's internal systems and their ability to function adequately.

Generosity/Service

The desire to share your unique gifts and skills with others as a way of serving humanity without expecting anything in return.

Growth/Expansion

To creatively enable an organisation to develop and expand.

Health/Healing/Harmony

To have a soundness of mind and body that flows from meeting your emotional and physical needs through self-awareness and disciplined preventive measures.

Hierarchy/Propriety/Order

To have a methodical, harmonious arrangement of persons and things, ranked above one another, in conformity with established standards of what is good and proper within an organisation.

Honour

To have high respect for the worth, merit or rank of those in authority, e.g. parents, superiors or national leaders.

Human dignity

The basic right of every human being to have respect and to have their basic needs met in a way that will allow them the opportunity to develop their potential.

Human rights/World order

To create the means for every person in the world to experience their basic right to life-giving resources such as food, shelter, employment, health and a minimal practical education.

Independence

To think and act for yourself in matters of opinion, conduct etc., without being subject to external constraint or authority.

Integration/Wholeness

To organise your personality (mind and body) into a coordinated, harmonious totality.

Interdependence

To value personal and inter-institutional cooperation above individual decision-making.

Intimacy

To be able to share yourself fully — thoughts, feelings, fantasies and realities — mutually and freely with another on a regular basis.

Intimacy/Solitude as unitive

To experience the personal harmony that results from a combination of meditative practice, mutual openness and total acceptance of another. The experience leads to new levels of meaning and awareness of truth.

Justice/Global distribution

To elicit inter-institutional and governmental collaboration to help provide the basic life necessities for the poor in the world.

Justice/Social order

To see every human being as being of equal value and to place a priority on taking a course of action that addresses, confronts and helps correct conditions of human oppression.

Knowledge/Discovery/Insight

To be motivated by the experience of moments of insight in a quest for truth through patterned investigation.

Law/Guide

To see authoritative principles and regulations as a means for creating your own criteria and moral conscience, and questioning those rules until they are clear and meaningful to you.

Law/Rule

To live life by the rules. To govern your conduct, action and procedures by the established legal system.

Leisure/Freesence

To use your time in a way that requires as much skill and concentration as your work, yet totally detaches you from work so that your spontaneous self is free to emerge in a playful and contagious manner.

Life/Self-actualisation

To experience and express the totality of your being through spiritual, psychological, physical and mental exercises with the goal of developing your full potential.

Limitation/Acceptance

To give positive acceptance to the fact that people have weaknesses and limitations. To see their limitations as a necessary consequence of their strengths.

Limitation/Celebration

To recognise that your limitations are part of the framework for exercising your talents. To have the ability to laugh at your own imperfections.

Loyalty/Fidelity

To see as important the strict observance of promises and duties to those in authority and to those in close personal relationships.

Macroeconomics/World order

To manage and direct the use of financial resources at an institutional and inter-institutional level. The goal being the creation of a more stable and equitable world economic order.

Management

To control and direct personnel in a business or institution for the purpose of optimal productivity and efficiency.

Membership/Institution

To take pride in belonging to and functioning as an integral part of an organisation, foundation, establishment, etc.

Minessence

To miniaturise and simplify complex ideas or technology into concrete and practical applications for the purpose of creatively impacting on the world-view of the user.

Mission/Objectives
To establish organisational goals and execute long term planning that takes into consideration the needs of society and how the organisation contributes to those needs.

Mutual responsibility/Accountability
To maintain a reciprocal balance of tasks and assignments with others so that everyone is answerable for their own area of responsibility.

Obedience/Duty
Dutiful and submissive compliance with moral and legal obligations established by parents, civic or religious authorities.

Obedience/Mutual accountability
To be mutually and equally responsible for establishing and complying to a common set of rules and guidelines in a group.

Ownership
Personal and legal possession of skills, decisions and property that gives you a sense of personal authority.

Patriotism/Esteem
To honour your country through personal devotion, love and support.

Personal authority/Honesty
To be in the position of being able to honestly express your full range of feelings and thoughts in a straightforward, objective manner. To command authority in your area of expertise.

Physical delight
To delight in the joy of experiencing the stimulation of all the senses of your body, e.g. having a massage, sunbathing, taking a spa bath.

Pioneerism/Innovation
To introduce and originate creative ideas for positive change in organisations and other social systems. To provide the framework for implementing them.

Play/Recreation
To engage in an undirected, spontaneous pastime or diversion from the anxiety of daily life. To 'recharge your batteries' through playful activities.

Presence/Dwelling
To be there for another person in such a way that, through your own self-knowledge and inner wisdom, they are able to perceive themselves with increased clarity.

Prestige/Image
To have a physical appearance which reflects your success and achievement, gains the esteem of others and promotes success.

Productivity
To feel energised by generating and completing tasks and activities. To be keen to achieve the goals set for you by others and to live up to their expectations.

Property/Control
To accumulate property, and exercise personal control over it, for your security and to meet your basic physical and emotional needs.

Prophet/Vision
To perceive, with clarity, global issues of social justice, human rights, ecology, etc. To communicate your vision in relation to these issues, with such clarity, that your listeners are empowered by it to take action.

Relaxation
A diversion from physical or mental work which reduces stress and provides a balance of work and play as a means of realising your potential.

Research/Originality/Knowledge
The systematic investigation and contemplation of the nature of truths and principles that lie behind our experience of reality. The aim is to create new insights and awareness — to see things as no one has before.

Responsibility
To be personally accountable for, and in charge of, a specific area or course of action in your group or organisation.

Rights/Respect
To respect the rights and property of others as you expect them to respect you and yours.

Ritual communication
To use liturgy and the arts as a communication medium for raising people's critical awareness of social issues.

Rule/Accountability
To have each person openly explain or justify their behaviour in relation to established codes of conduct, procedures, standards, etc.

Safety/Survival
To avoid personal injury, danger, or loss, and to do what is necessary to protect yourself in adverse circumstances.

Search/Meaning/Hope
The inner longing and curiosity to integrate your feelings, imagination and knowledge in order to discover your unique place in the world. To search for 'your place in the scheme of things'.

Security
To have a safe place or relationship where you experience protection and freedom from cares and anxieties. A place you find comforting to have.

Self-interest/Control
To restrain your feelings and control your personal interests for the purpose of physical survival in this world.

Self-preservation
To do whatever is necessary to protect yourself from physical harm or destruction in what you perceive as an alien/threatening world. To look after 'number one' in the face of threat.

Self-worth
The knowledge that when those you respect and esteem really know you, they will affirm you are worthy of their respect.

Sensory pleasure/Sexuality
To gratify your sensual desires and fully express your sexuality.

Service/Vocation
To use your unique gifts, skills and abilities to contribute to society through your occupation, business, profession or calling.

Sharing/Listening/Trust
To actively and accurately hear and sense another's thoughts and feelings. To express your own thoughts and feelings in a climate of mutual trust and confidence in each other's integrity.

Simplicity/Play
To have a deep appreciation of the world combined with a playful attitude toward organisations and systems that people find energising and positive. To see simplicity in complexity and to be detached from the material world.

Social affirmation
Personal respect and validation, arising from the support and respect of your peers, which is necessary for your growth and success.

Support/Peer
To be sustained in both joyful and difficult times, by persons similar to yourself.

Synergy
The harmonious and energising relationship of persons in a group that results in the group far surpassing its predicted ability (based on the summation of the abilities of its individual members).

Technology/Science
Systematic knowledge of the physical or natural world and practical applications of the knowledge through the construction of devices and tools.

Territory/Security
To make provision for physically defending your property, state or nation.

Tradition
To ritualise family history, religious history, or national history in your life so as to enrich its meaning. To pass on traditional ways through ritual and ceremony.

Transcendence/Global equality
To transcend physical needs with the intention of influencing issues of equality. For example a hunger strike to change the conditions for the inmates in a prison.

Truth/Wisdom/Integrated insight
The intense pursuit and discovery of ultimate truth above all other activities. To seek the wisdom that stems from understanding a set of universal principles that govern all things.

Unity/Diversity
To value groups, organisations, society and the ecosystem, that have a diversity of membership. To value biodiversity.

Unity/Uniformity
To create harmony and agreement in an institution to the end of achieving efficiency, order, loyalty and conformity to established norms.

Wonder/Awe/Fate
To be filled with marvel, amazement and awe when faced with the overwhelming grandeur and power of your physical environment. To feel that, at times, things are out of your hands and fate rules.

Wonder/Curiosity/Nature

To experience the physical world with marvel and wonder. To seek to learn about and explore it personally.

Word

The desire to communicate universal truths so effectively that the listeners become conscious of their strengths and limitations and life and hope are renewed for the individual.

Work/Labour

To have the skills and rights enabling you to produce an adequate living for yourself and your family.

Workmanship/Craft/Art

To create products or works of art to enhance the world and our life in it.

Worship/Faith/Creed

Reverence for and belief in God that is expressed and experienced through a commitment to religious doctrines and teachings.

Bibliography and recommended reading

Allport, G., *Pattern and Growth in Personality*, Holt Rinehart and Winston, New York, 1961

Barker, J., *Future edge: Discovering the New Paradigm of Success*, William Morrow and Company Inc, New York, 1992.

Barrett, R., *Liberating the Corporate Soul: Building a visionary organisation*, Butterworth Heinemann, Woburn MA, 1998.

Bateson, G., *Steps to an Ecology of Mind*, Ballantine Books, New York, 1972.

Blanchard, K., and O'Connor, M., *Managing by Values*, Berrett-Koehhler Publishers Inc, San Francisco, 1997.

Brooks, I., *Second to None: Six strategies for creating superior customer value*. Nahanni Publishing Ltd, Auckland, 1997.

Chippendale, P., and Colins, C., *New Wisdom II: Values Based Development*, Acorn Publications, Brisbane, 1995.

Clutterbuck, D. and Goldsmith, W., *The Winning Streak Mark 2*, Orion Business Books, London, 1998.

Collins, J., 'Aligning Action and Values', *Leader to Leader*, Drucker Foundation and Jossey Bass Inc, 1996.

Collins, J. and Porras, J., *Built to Last: Successful habits of visionary companies*, Random House, London, 1998.

Cook, D., McGuire, R., and Vernacchia, R., *Coaching Mental Excellence: It does matter whether you win or lose*, Warde Publishers, California, 1996.

Cooper, R., and Sawaf, A., *Executive EQ: Emotional intelligence in business*, Orion Business Books, London, 1997.

Covey, S., *The Seven Habits of Highly Effective People*, Simon and Schuster, New York, 1990.

Csikszentmihalyi, M., *Finding Flow: The psychology of engagement with everyday life*, HarperCollins, New York, 1997.

Csikszentmihalyi, M., *Flow: the psychology of happiness*, Rider, London, 1992.

Dilts, R., *Visionary Leadership Skills: Creating a world to which people want to belong*, Meta Publications, California, 1996.

Elkington, J., *Cannibals with Forks: The triple bottom line of 21st century business*, Capstone Publishing, Oxford, 1997.

Endenburg, G., *Sociocracy as Social Design*, E Buron, Rotterdam, 1998.

Fritz, R., *The Path of Least Resistance for Managers: Learning to become the creative force in your life*, Ballantine, Inc, New York, 1989.

Fritz, R., *The Path of Least Resistance for Managers: Designing organisations to succeed*, Berrett-Koehler Publishers, Inc, San Francisco, 1999.

Garratt, B., *The Learning Organization: Developing democracy at work*, HarperCollins, London, 2000.

Glasser, W., *Control Theory: A new explanation of how we control our lives*, Harper & Row, New York, 1984.

Hampden-Turner, C., and Trompenaars, A., *The Seven Cultures of Capitalism*, Doubleday, New York, 1993.

Harker, P., and Scott, T., *The Myth of the Nine to Five: Work, workplaces and the workplace relationships*, Shannon Books, Victoria, 2002.

Henderson, M., *Finding True North: Discover your values, enrich your life*, HarperCollins, Auckland, 2003.

Hilliard, A., *The Forms of Value: The extension of a hedonistic axiology*, Columbia Universtity Press, New York, 1950.

Holdsworth, L., *A New Generation of Business Leaders*, Holdsworth Press, Christchurch, 2000.

Holland, G., *A Call for Connection: Solutions for creating a whole new culture*, New World Library, Florida, 1998.

Japp, T., *Enabling Leadership: Achieving results with people*, HRA Publications, London, 1986.

Jones, R., *The Big Idea*, HarperCollins, London, 2000.

Kelly, A., and Sewell, S., *With Head Heart and Hands: Dimensions of community building*. Boolarong Publications, Bowen Hills, 1988.

Kluckhohn, C., *Values and Value Orientation in the Theory of Action*, Greenwood Press, Cambridge Mass, 1951.

Koch, R., *The 80/20 Principle: The secret of achieving more with less*, Nicholas Brealey Limited, London, 1998.

Konorski, J., *Integrative Activity of the Brain*, Chicago Press, Chicago, 1967.

Kotter, J. and Heskett, J., *Corporate Culture and Performance*, Free Press, Boston, 1992.

Landsberg, M., *The Tao of Coaching: Boost your effectiveness at work by inspiring and developing those around you*, HarperCollins, London, 1996.

Maslon, A., *Farther Reaches of Human Nature*, Viking Press, New York, 1971.

Miller, W., *Flash of Brilliance: Inspiring creativity where you work*. Perseus Books, New York, 1999.

Mitroff, I. and Denton, E., *A Spiritual Audit of Corporate America: A hard look at spirituality, religion, and values in the workplace*, Jossey-Bass Inc, San Francisco, 1999.

Molden, D., *Managing with the Power of NLP. Neuro-linguistic programming for competitive advantage*, Financial Times Prentice Hall, London, 1996.

Najder, Z., *Values and Evaluation*, Oxford University Press, Oxford, 1975.

O'Reilly, C., and Pfeffer, J., *Hidden Value: How great companies achieve extraordinary results with ordinary people*, Harvard Business School Press, Boston, 2000.

Palmer, H., *Resurfacing*, Stars Edge International, Florida, 1994.

Persig, R., *Lila: an inquiry into morals*, Corgi, London, 1992.

Peters, T. and Waterman, R., *In Search of Excellence: Lessons from America's best-run companies*, Harper and Row, New York, 1982.

Posner, B., and Schmidt, W., 'Values Congruence and Differences Between the Interplay of Personal and Organisational Values Systems', *Journal of Business Ethics*, 341–347, 1993.

Ray, P. and Anderson, S., *The Cultural Creatives: How 50 million people are changing the world*, Three Rivers Press, Michigan, 2001.

Roddick, A., *Business as Unusual: The triumph of Anita Roddick*, HarperCollins, London, 2000.

Rokeach, M., *The Nature of Human Values*, Free Press, New York, 1973.

Scott, T. and Harker, P., *Humanity at Work*, Phil Harker & Associates Pty Ltd, Queensland, 1998.

Secretan, L., *Reclaiming Higher Ground: Creating organisations that inspire the soul*, McGraw-Hill, New York, 1997.

Secretan, L., *The Way of the Tiger: Gentle wisdom for turbulent times*, The Thaler Corporation Inc, Ontario, 1998.

Senge, P., *The Fifth Discipline*, Random House, Sydney, 1992.

Thompson, K., *Emotional Capital: Capturing hearts and minds to create lasting business success*, Capstone Publishing, Oxford, 2000.

Tosey, P. and Smith, P., 'Assessing the Learning Organization: Part 2 — exploring practical assessment processes', *The Learning Organization: An international journal*, Vol 6, No 3, 107–115.

Wheatley, M., *Leadership and the New Science: Learning about organisation from an orderly universe*, Berrett-Koehler, San Francisco, 2001.

Whitmore, J., *Coaching for Performance*, Nicholas Brealey, London, 1996.

Wilk Braksick, L., *Unlock Behavior, Unleash Profits: How your leadership behaviour can unlock profitability in your organisation*, McGraw Hill, New York, 2000.

Wright, K., *Breaking the Rules: Removing the obstacles to effortless high performance*, CPM Publishing, Boise, 1998.

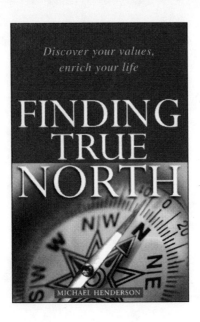

Finding True North

Ever feel like you're working harder than ever, but don't know why? Is balancing your lifestyle exhausting you? Worried you're busy climbing the ladder but it's leaning against the wrong wall?

The first step towards a successful life is knowing what's important to *you*. When you know what that is, you can then focus your efforts on achieving what matters, instead of jumping at the next chance that comes along.

Michael Henderson, accredited values coach and director of Values at Work, has written a practical, step-by-step guide to help you clarify and prioritise the most important things in *your* life. He has helped thousands of people to define and apply their values in their daily lives, and his clear, user-friendly approach will help you to do the same.

Harper*Business*
An imprint of HarperCollins*Publishers*

Speak Easy

In her many years as a communications consultant, media trainer and performer, Maggie Eyre has developed a thorough understanding of what is involved in public speaking. Whether you are facing a business presentation or an after-dinner speech, Maggie can guide you from initial concept to final delivery. Included in *Speak Easy* are chapters on body language, voice, health, warming up, managing your audience, fear, media skills, grooming and learning your lines. Along the way Maggie recounts many anecdotes and case studies based on her own work and experience, with useful tips and summaries. This practical and authoritative handbook is destined to become the manual of choice for anyone looking to improve their public speaking and presentation skills.

HarperCollins*Publishers*

Who Says Elephants Can't Dance?

Who Says Elephants Can't Dance? tells the story of IBM's competitive and cultural transformation. In his own words, Gerstner offers a blow-by-blow account of his arrival at the company and his campaign to rebuild the leadership team and give the workforce a renewed sense of purpose. In the process, Gerstner defined a strategy for the computing giant and remade the ossified culture bred by the company's own success.

The first-hand story of an extraordinay turnaround, a unique case study in managing a crisis, and a thoughtful reflection on the computer industry and the principles of leadership, *Who Says Elephants Can't Dance?* sums up Lou Gerstner's historic business achievement. Gerstner recounts the high-level meetings and explains the pressure-filled, no-turning-back decisions that had to be made. He also offers his hard-won conclusions about the essence of what makes a great company run.

Harper*Business*
An imprint of HarperCollins*Publishers*

How to Mind Map®

Mind Mapping is a revolutionary system of planning and note-taking that has changed the lives of millions of people across the world. *How to Mind Map*® is the definitive guide to Mind Maps®, brought to you by their inventor, Tony Buzan. This practical pocket guide explains how Mind Maps make it easy to:
- plan a presentation or a report
- think up brilliant ideas
- persuade people and negotiate
- remember things
- plan personal goals
- gain control of your life

 Thorsens

The Power of Verbal Intelligence

With Tony Buzan's help, you need never be lost for words ever again!
This book shows you how to harness the power of your verbal
intelligence and become brilliant with words — reading, speaking,
remembering and understanding them — improving your social life
and your career in the bargain! This book includes Buzan's
revolutionary techniques for improving recall and understanding and
shows you how to:

- increase your vocabulary, your creativity and memory
- use Mind Maps® to develop your word power
- improve your comprehension
- become a successful conversationalist and speaker

 Thorsens